PIANO / VOCAL / GUITAR

TOP CHRISTIAN HITS
OF 2022-2023
← ≪ 14 UPLIFTING SONGS ≫ →

ISBN 978-1-70518-869-9

Visit Hal Leonard Online at
www.halleonard.com

World headquarters, contact:
Hal Leonard
7777 West Bluemound Road
Milwaukee, WI 53213
Email: info@halleonard.com

In Europe, contact:
Hal Leonard Europe Limited
1 Red Place
London, W1K 6PL
Email: info@halleonardeurope.com

In Australia, contact:
Hal Leonard Australia Pty. Ltd.
4 Lentara Court
Cheltenham, Victoria, 3192 Australia
Email: info@halleonard.com.au

CONTENTS

ALWAYS

Words and Music by CHRIS TOMLIN,
JEFF SOJKA, BEN GLOVER,
JESS CATES and DANIEL CARSON

I will tell of Your won - ders, sing of Your grace. __ The

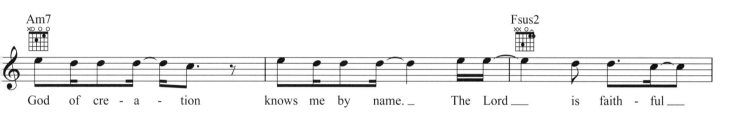

God of cre - a - tion knows me by name. __ The Lord __ is faith - ful __

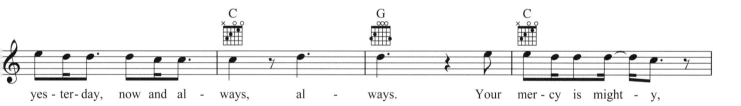

yes - ter - day, now and al - ways, al - ways. Your mer - cy is might - y,

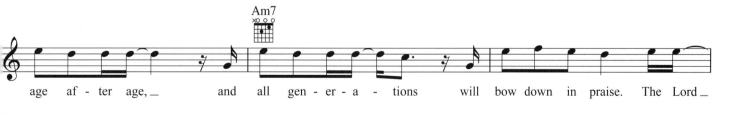

age af - ter age, __ and all gen - er - a - tions will bow down in praise. The Lord __

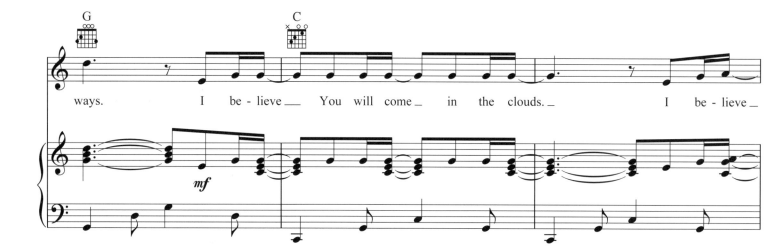

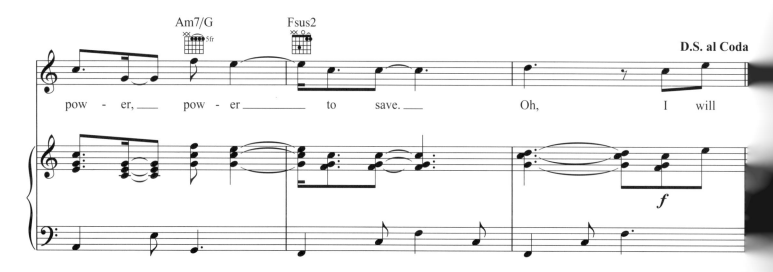

CODA

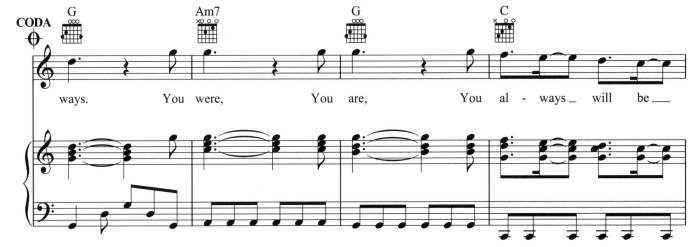

ways. You were, You are, You al - ways_ will be_

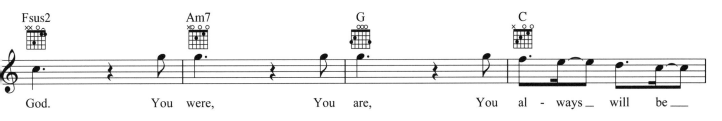

God. You were, You are, You al - ways_ will be_

God. Yes, You al - ways_ will be_ God. I will

tell of Your won - ders, sing of Your grace._ The God of cre - a - tion

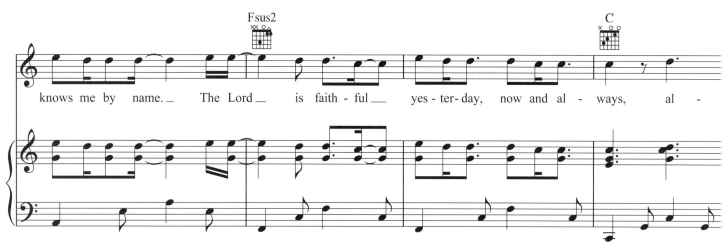

knows me by name.___ The Lord___ is faith - ful___ yes - ter-day, now and al - ways, al -

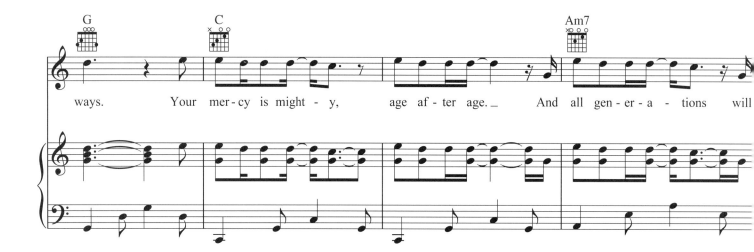

ways. Your mer-cy is might - y, age af - ter age.___ And all gen-er-a - tions will

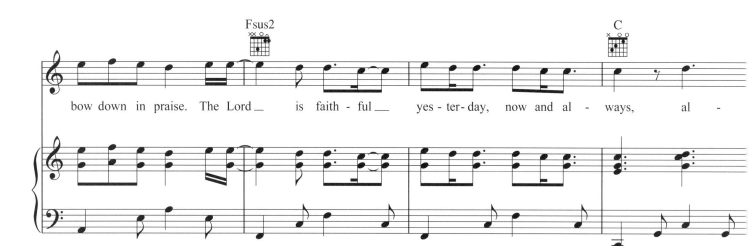

bow down in praise. The Lord___ is faith - ful___ yes - ter-day, now and al - ways, al -

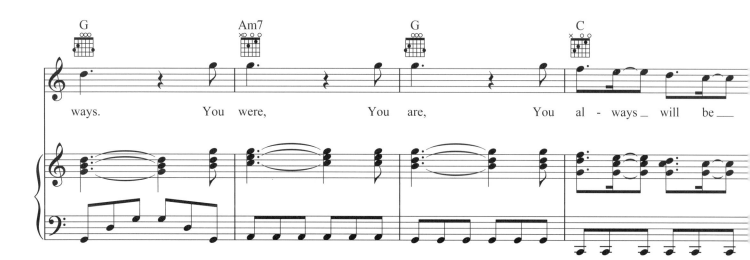

ways. You were, You are, You al - ways___ will be___

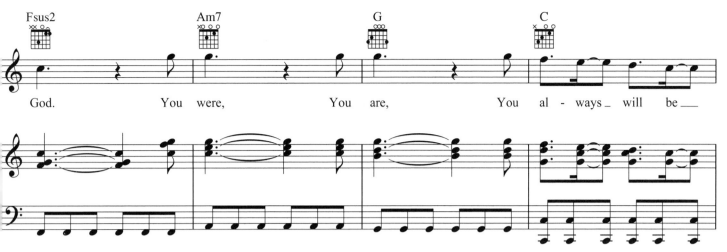

God. You were, You are, You al - ways _ will be _

God. Oh, You al - ways _ will be _ God. Your

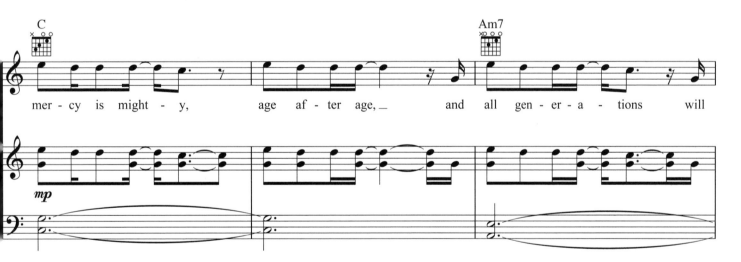

mer - cy is might - y, age af - ter age, _ and all gen - er - a - tions will

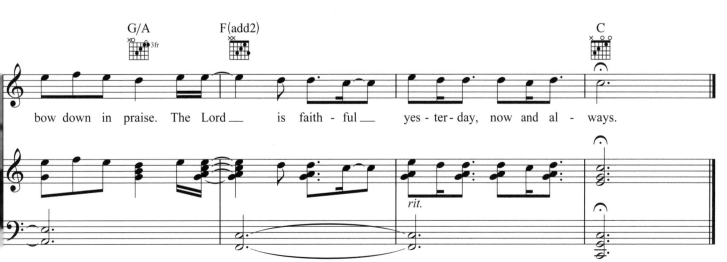

bow down in praise. The Lord _ is faith - ful _ yes - ter - day, now and al - ways.

BRIGHTER DAYS

Words and Music by SAM ELLIS
and BLESSING OFFOR

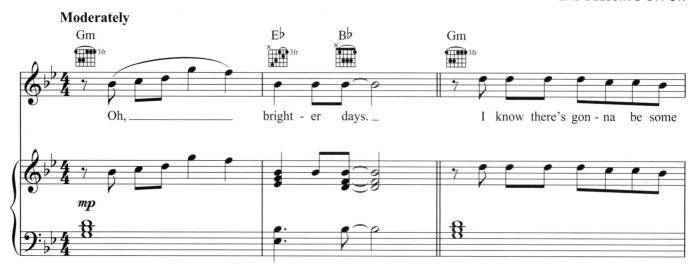

Oh, _____ bright-er days. _ I know there's gon-na be some

bright-er days. _ I swear that love will find you in your pain. _

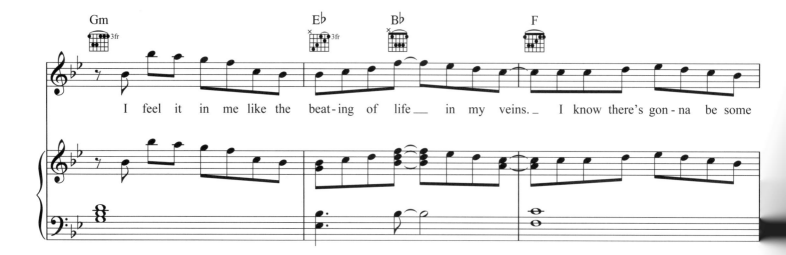

I feel it in me like the beat-ing of life _ in my veins. _ I know there's gon-na be some

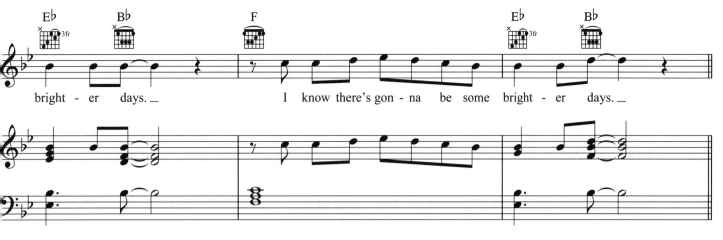

bright - er days. _ I know there's gon - na be some bright - er days. _

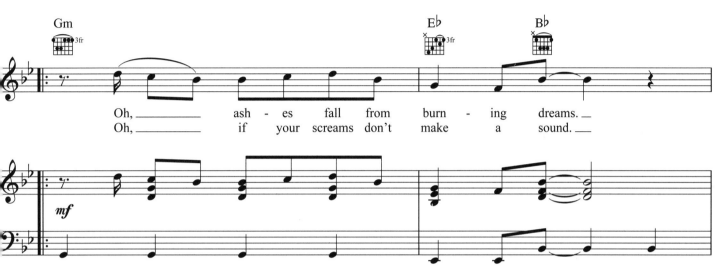

Oh, _____ ash - es fall from burn - ing dreams. _
Oh, _____ if your screams don't make a sound. _

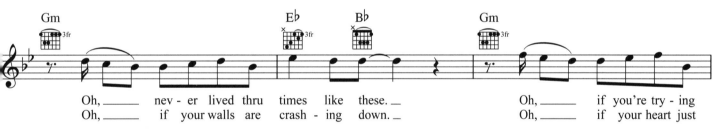

Oh, _____ nev - er lived thru times like these. _ Oh, _____ if you're try - ing
Oh, _____ if your walls are crash - ing down. _ Oh, _____ if your heart just

hard to breathe, _ in the dark, ___ in the dark: _____ }
cries too loud ___ all the time, ___ all the time: _____ }

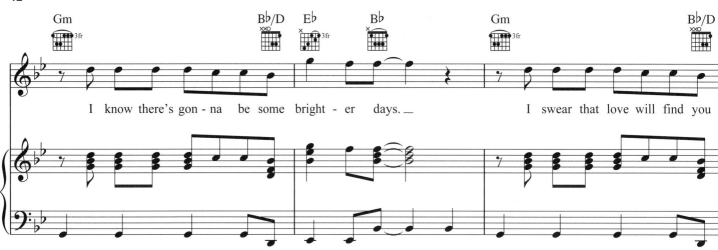

I know there's gon-na be some bright-er days. __ I swear that love will find you

in your pain. __ I feel it in me like the beat-ing of life __ in my veins.

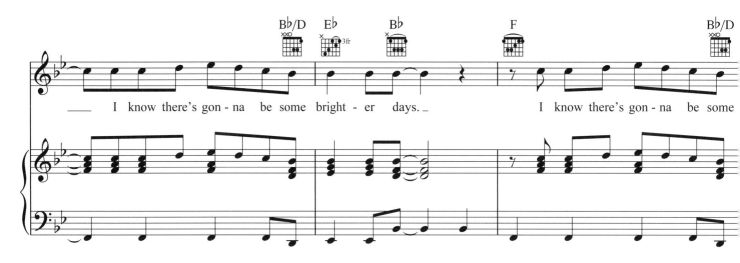

__ I know there's gon-na be some bright-er days. _ I know there's gon-na be some

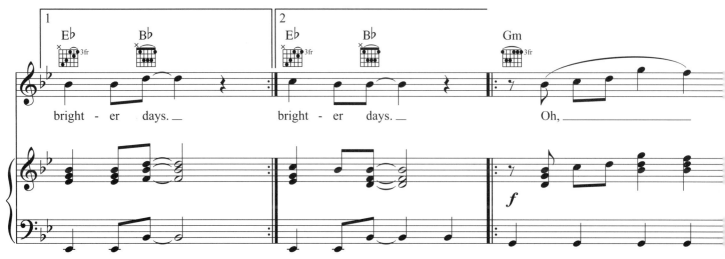

1 bright-er days. __ **2** bright-er days. __ Oh, _____

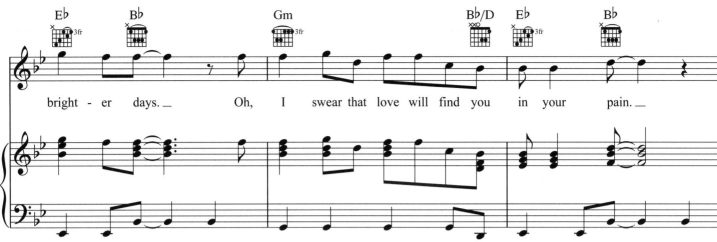

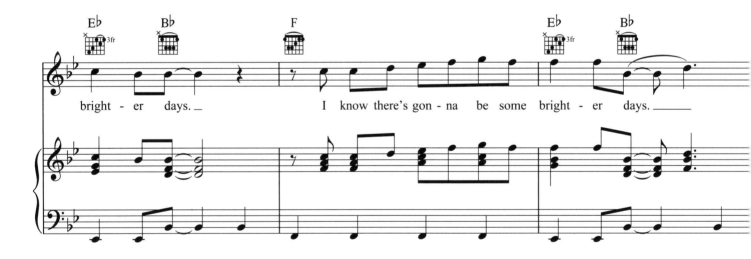

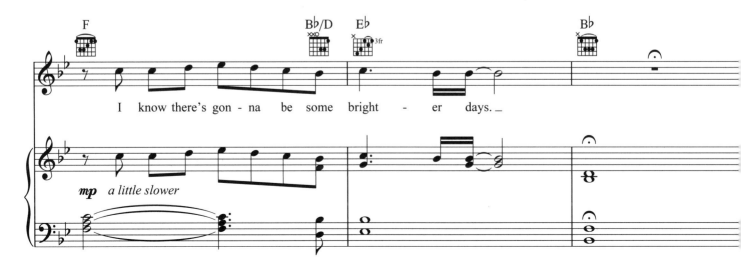

FILL MY CUP

Words and Music by ANDREW RIPP,
ETHAN HULSE and THAD COCKRELL

Moderate Rock beat

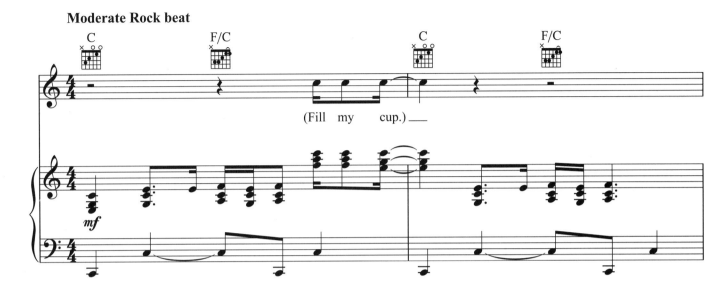

(Fill my cup.) —

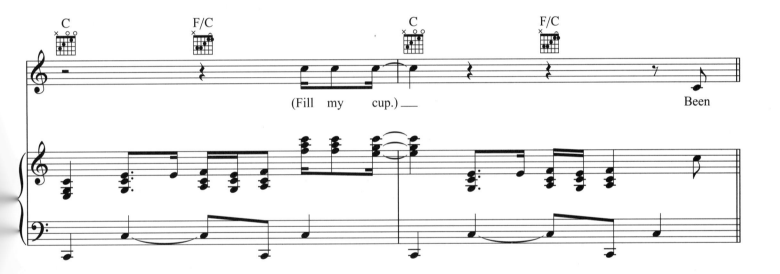

(Fill my cup.) — Been

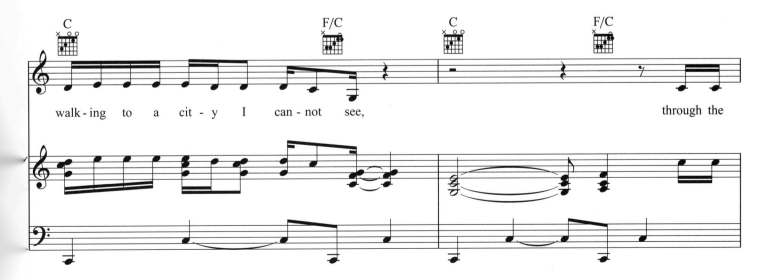

walk-ing to a cit-y I can-not see, through the

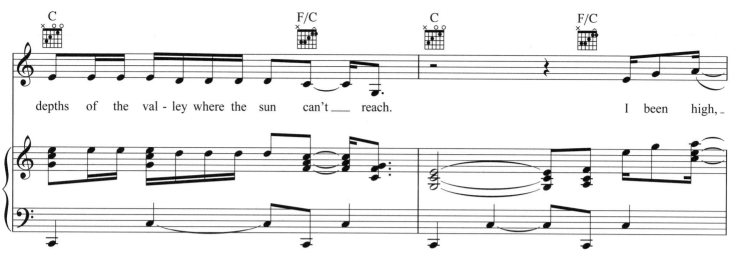

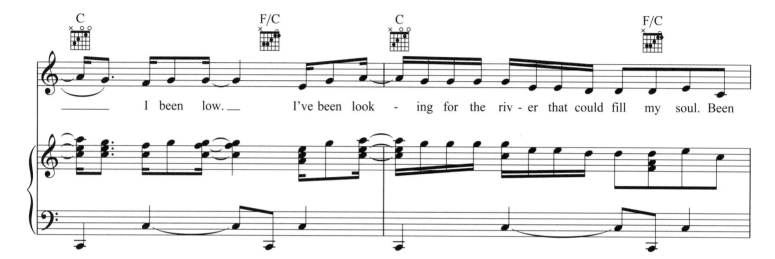

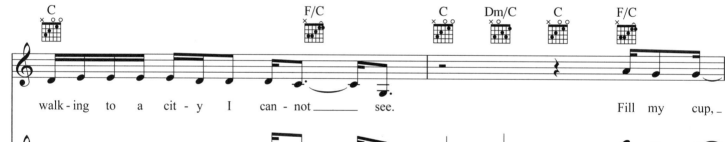

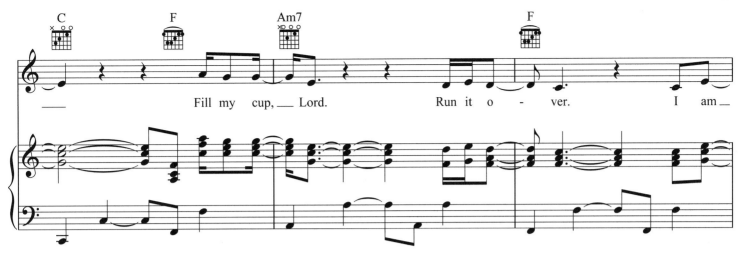

Fill my cup, ___ Lord. Run it o - ver. I am ___

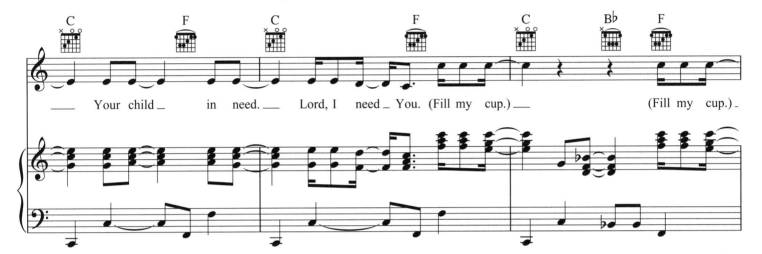

___ Your child ___ in need. ___ Lord, I need ___ You. (Fill my cup.) ___ (Fill my cup.) ___

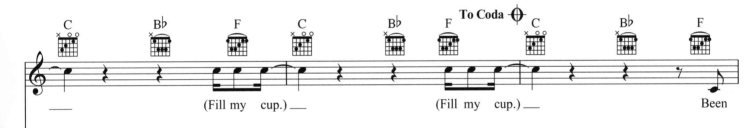

To Coda ⊕

___ (Fill my cup.) ___ (Fill my cup.) ___ Been

walk - ing o - ver lies stand - ing in my ___ way. They can

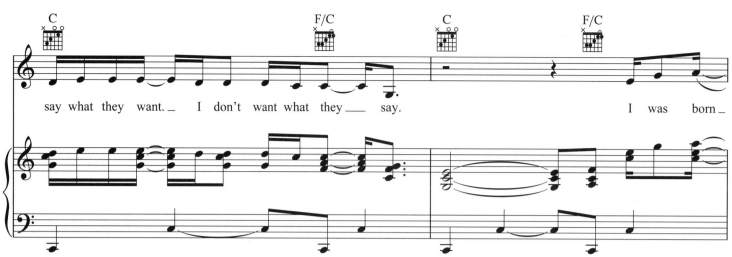

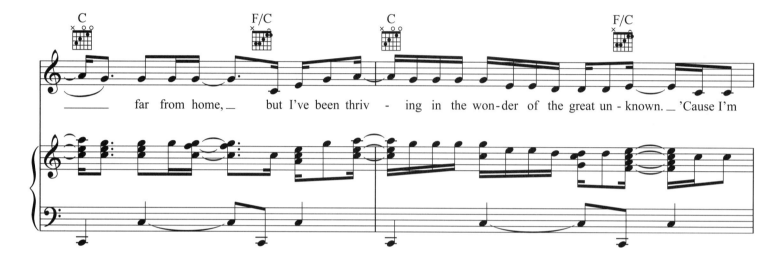

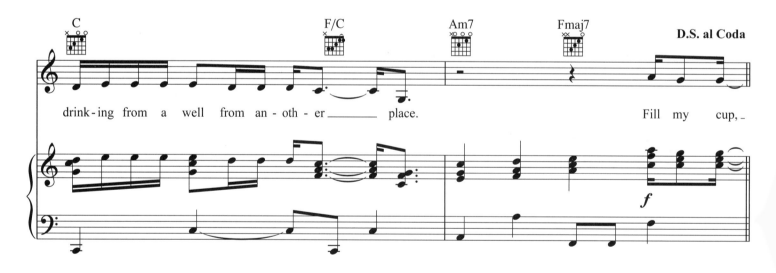

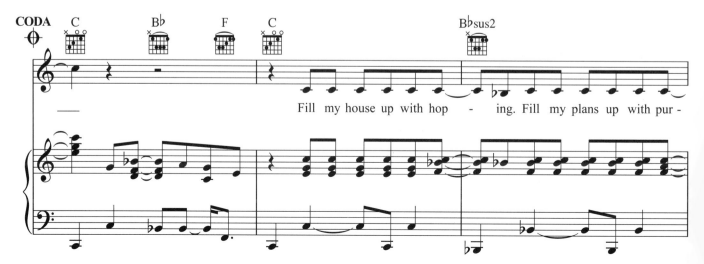

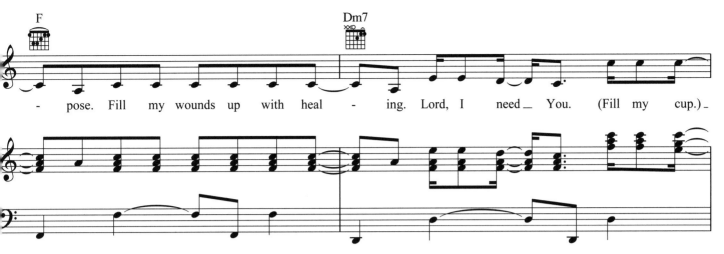

- pose. Fill my wounds up with heal - ing. Lord, I need__ You. (Fill my cup.)__

___ Fill my days up with mean - ing. Fill my fu - ture with vi - sion, good - ness, grace and pro - vi -

- sion. Lord, I need__ You. And when I get to that cit - y I can - not___ see,

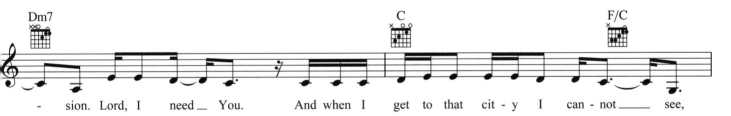

I'll know that e - ven this val - ley was a gold - en___ street.

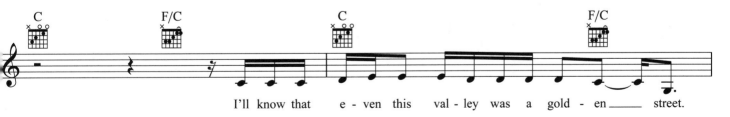

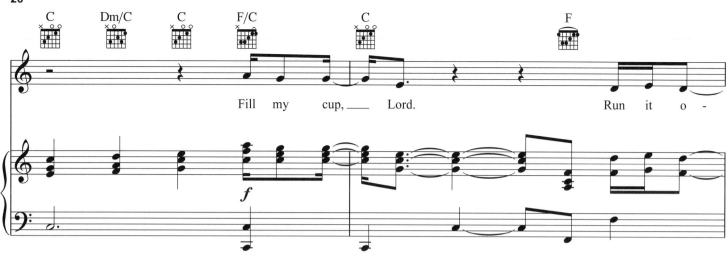

Fill my cup, ___ Lord.   Run it o-

-ver.   Give me love, ___ give me joy, ___ give me peace. ___

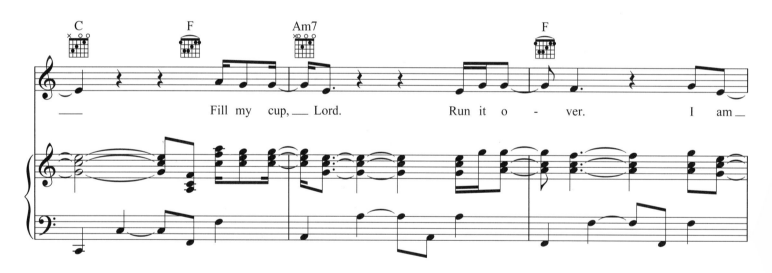

___   Fill my cup, ___ Lord.   Run it o-ver.   I am

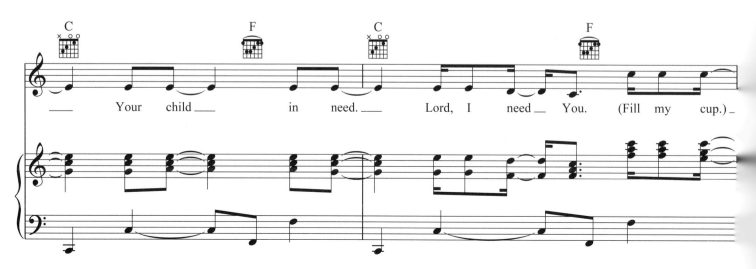

___ Your child ___ in need. ___ Lord, I need ___ You. (Fill my cup.) ___

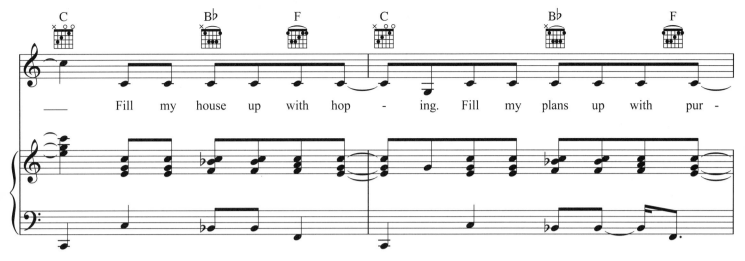

Fill my house up with hop — ing. Fill my plans up with pur —

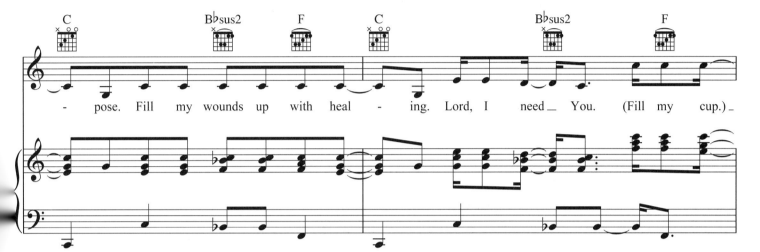

- pose. Fill my wounds up with heal — ing. Lord, I need _ You. (Fill my cup.) _

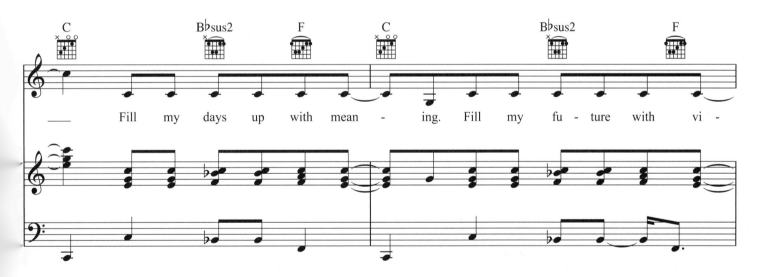

_ Fill my days up with mean — ing. Fill my fu - ture with vi —

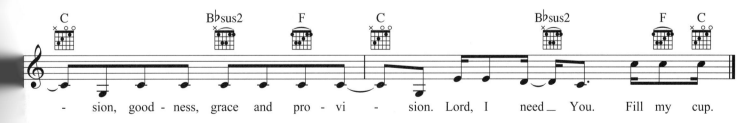

- sion, good - ness, grace and pro - vi - sion. Lord, I need _ You. Fill my cup.

BUILD A BOAT

Words and Music by PETE BECKER,
SETH MOSLEY, JOHAN LINDBRANT,
COLTON DIXON, MIKEY GORMLEY
and SANDRO CAVAZZA

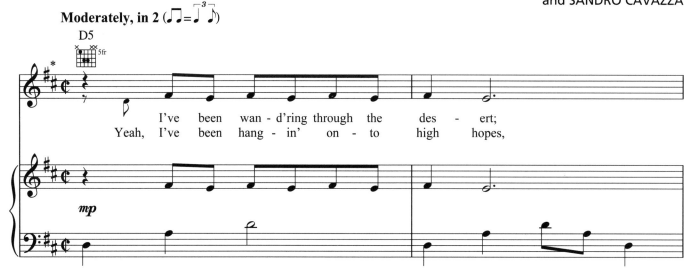

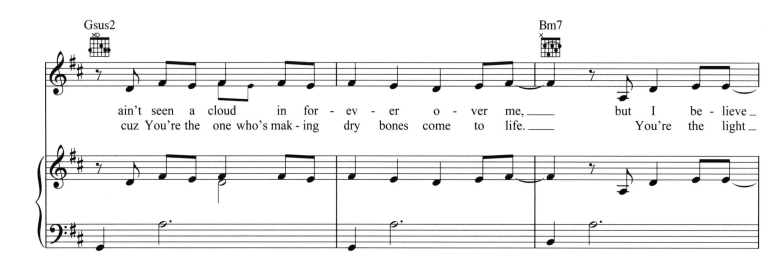

Recorded a half step lower.

Ev - 'ry word You say is gon - na come true. You will lead me to the prom - ised land. _

Ev - 'ry-thing You said's gon - na hap - pen, e - ven though I

have - n't seen it yet. _____ I will build a boat in the sand where they

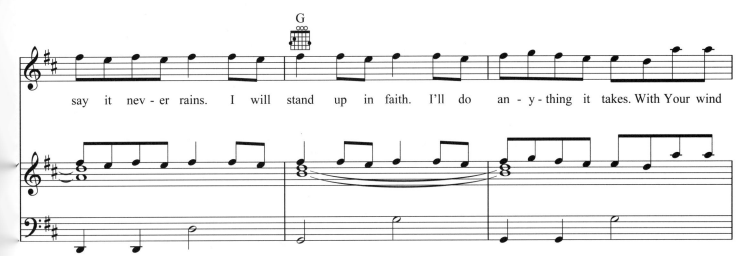

say it nev - er rains. I will stand up in faith. I'll do an - y - thing it takes. With Your wind

in my sails, __ Your love nev - er fails __ or fades. _____ I'll build a

boat in the des - ert place, __ and when the flood and the wa - ter starts to rise, __ yeah,

I'll ride the storm, cuz I got You by my side. With your wind in my sails, __ Your love

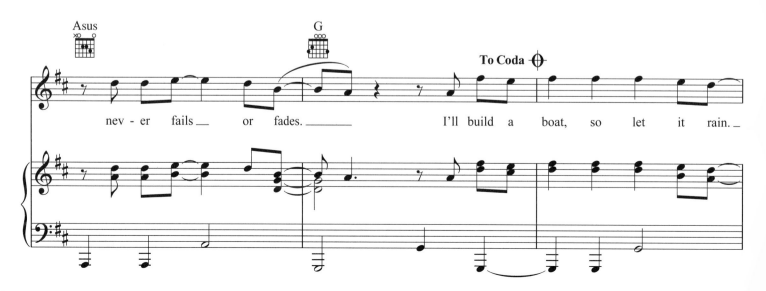

To Coda ⊕

nev - er fails __ or fades. _____ I'll build a boat, so let it rain. __

You're the map, You're my com- pass.

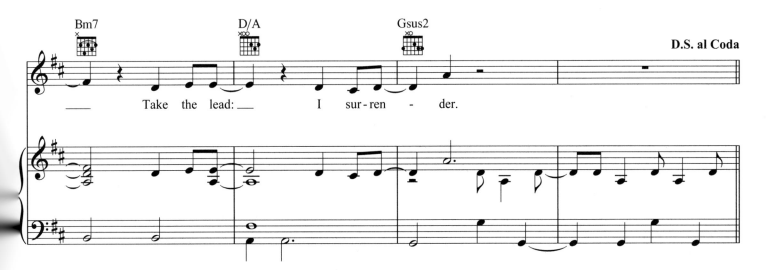

You help me nav - i - gate the cur - rents un - der me. Take the lead: __ I sur - ren - der.

D.S. al Coda

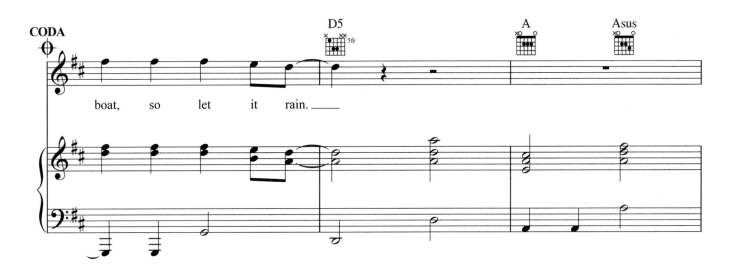

CODA

boat, so let it rain. __

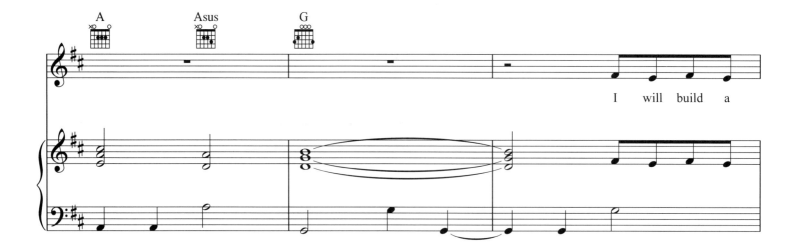

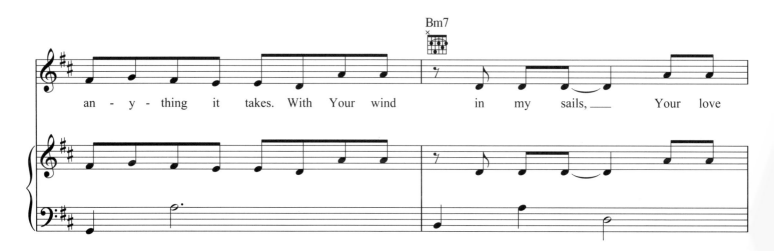

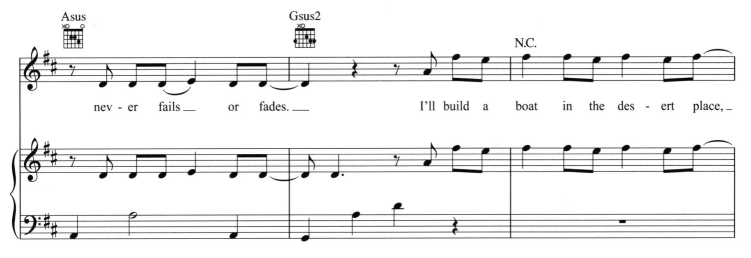

nev - er fails __ or fades. __ I'll build a boat in the des - ert place, __

__ and when the flood and the wa - ter starts to rise, __ yeah, I'll ride the storm, cuz I

got You by my side. With Your wind in my sails, _ Your love nev - er fails __ or fades. _

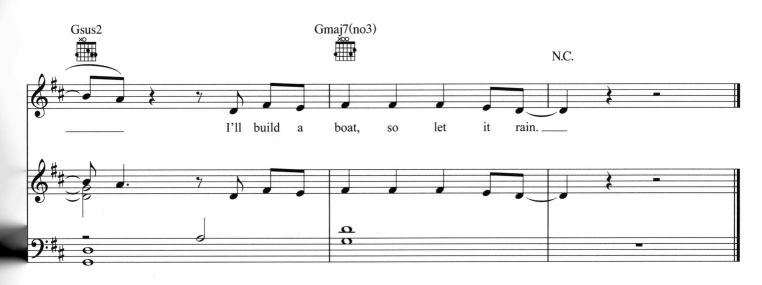

_____ I'll build a boat, so let it rain. __

GETTING STARTED

Words and Music by JEREMY CAMP,
RAN JACKSON and RICKY JACKSON

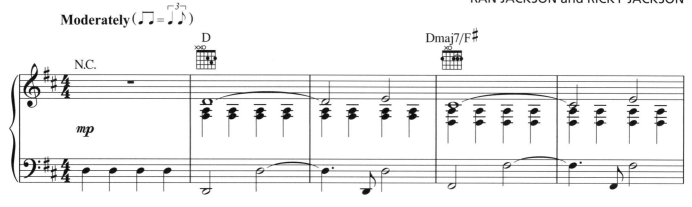

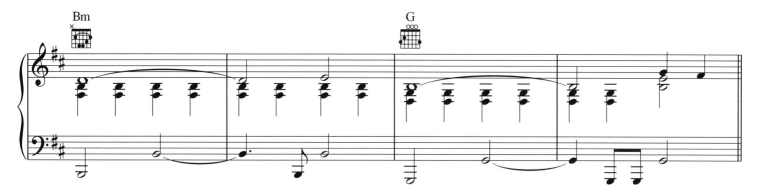

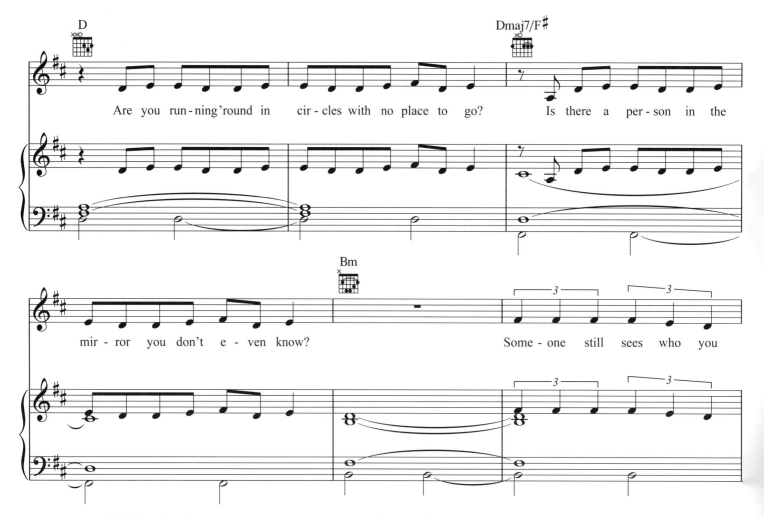

Are you run-ning 'round in cir-cles with no place to go? Is there a per-son in the mir-ror you don't e-ven know? Some-one still sees who you

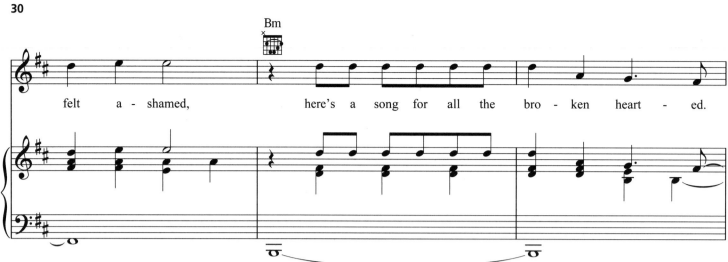

felt a - shamed, here's a song for all the bro - ken heart - ed.

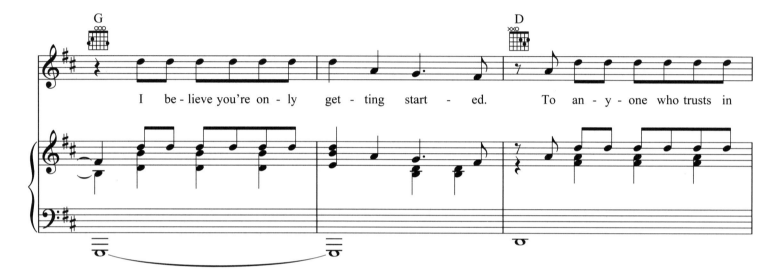

I be - lieve you're on - ly get - ting start - ed. To an - y - one who trusts in

Je - sus' name, watch your world be - come for - ev - er changed.

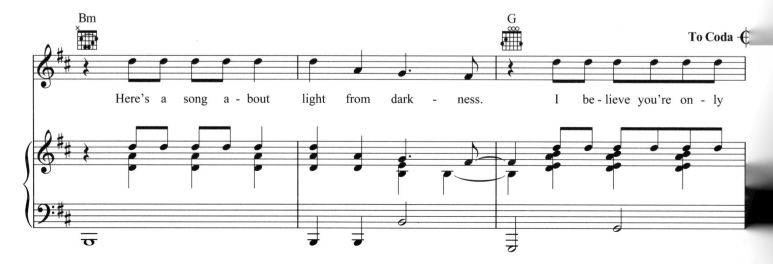

Here's a song a - bout light from dark - ness. I be - lieve you're on - ly

To Coda

Fall in his arms and let him wash you clean. He'll tear off the chains so that

you can be free. New love be-gins and the old is re-deemed.

D.S. al Coda

Oh, I be-lieve, _____ yeah.

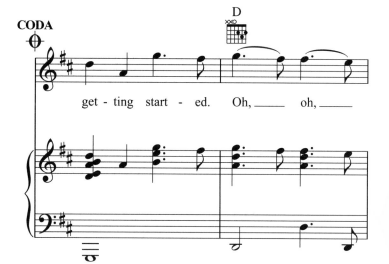

CODA

get-ting start-ed. Oh, _____ oh,

oh, _____ oh. Oh, _____ oh, _____ oh. Oh, _____ oh, He

loves you, He loves you, He   loves you.   Oh, _____ oh, _____

oh, _____ oh. _____   Oh, _____ oh, _____ whoa, _____ whoa.   Oh, _____ oh,   He

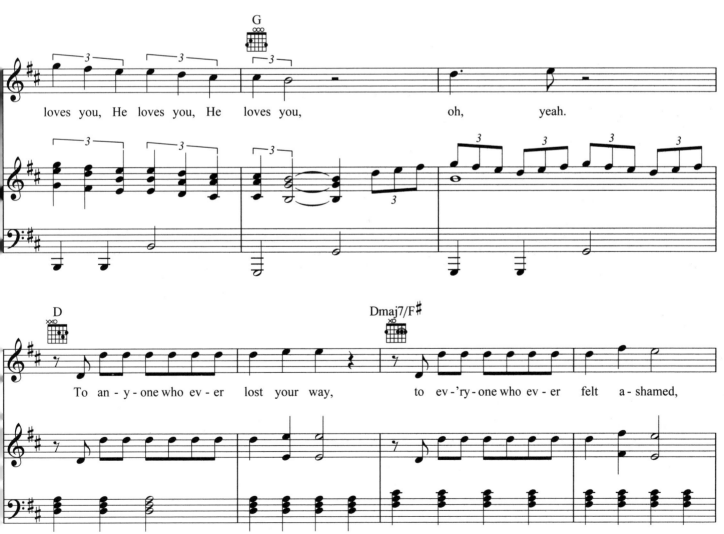

loves you, He loves you, He   loves you,   oh,   yeah.

To an - y - one who ev - er   lost your way,   to ev - 'ry - one who ev - er   felt a - shamed,

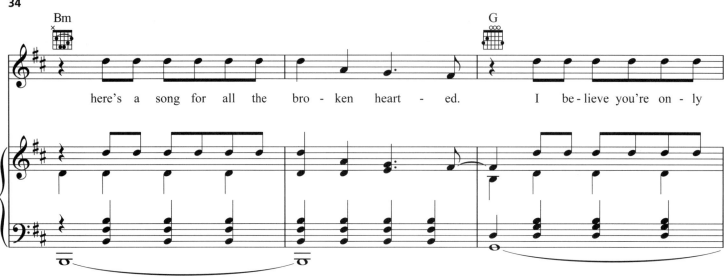

here's a song for all the bro-ken heart-ed. I be-lieve you're on-ly

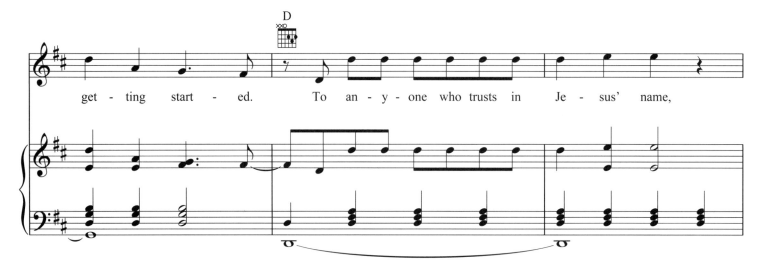

get-ting start-ed. To an-y-one who trusts in Je-sus' name,

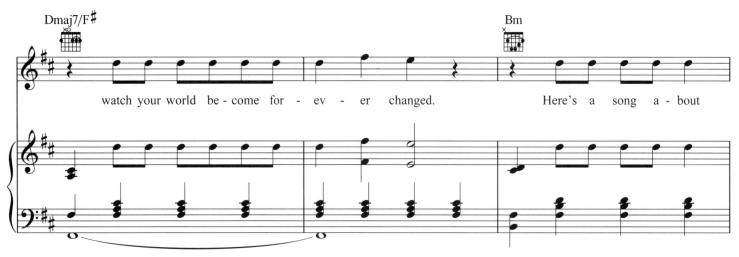

watch your world be-come for-ev-er changed. Here's a song a-bout

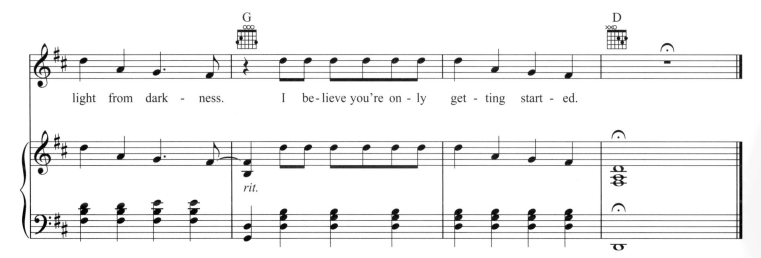

light from dark-ness. I be-lieve you're on-ly get-ting start-ed.

rit.

GOD IS IN THIS STORY

Words and Music by JEFF PARDO,
KATY NICHOLE and ETHAN HULSE

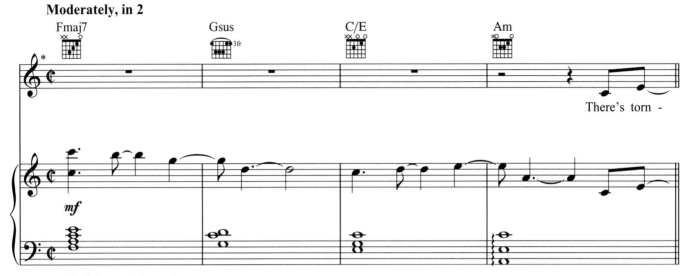

Pedal ad lib. throughout

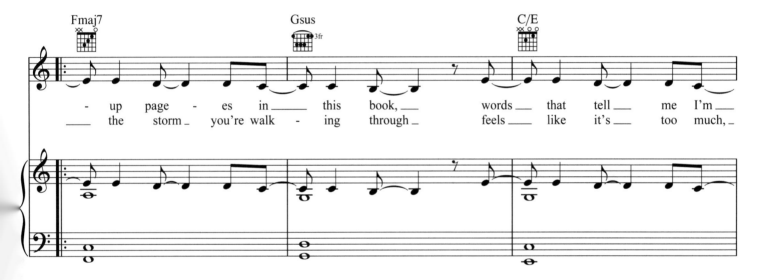

- up pag - es in ___ this book, ___ words ___ that tell ___ me I'm
___ the storm ___ you're walk - ing through ___ feels ___ like it's ___ too much, ___

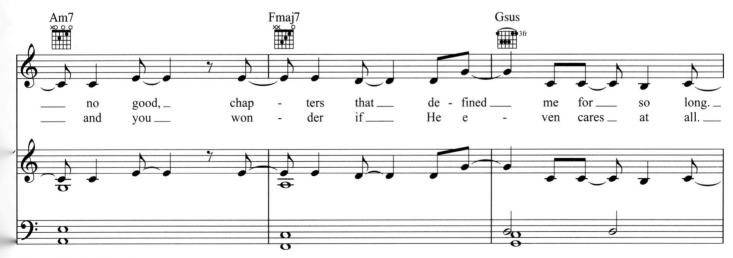

___ no good, ___ chap - ters that ___ de - fined ___ me for ___ so long. ___
___ and you ___ won - der if ___ He e - ven cares ___ at all. ___

Recorded a half step lower.

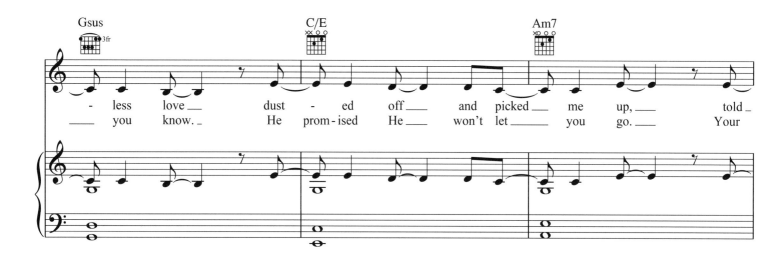

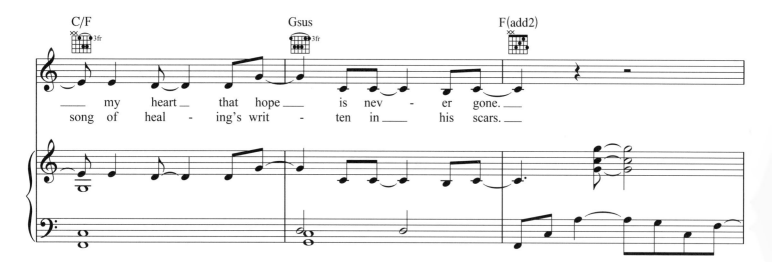

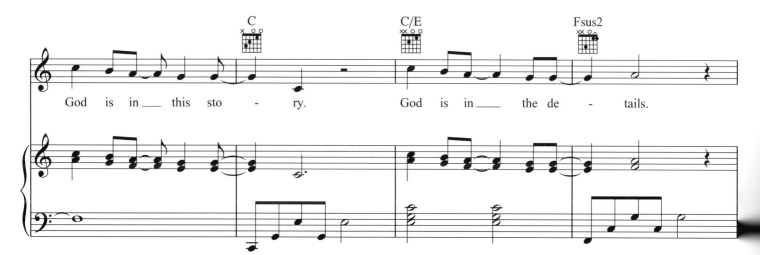

E- ven in ___ the bro - ken parts ___ he holds ___ my heart. __ He nev-

- er fails. _ When I'm at ___ my weak - est, I will trust __ in Je-

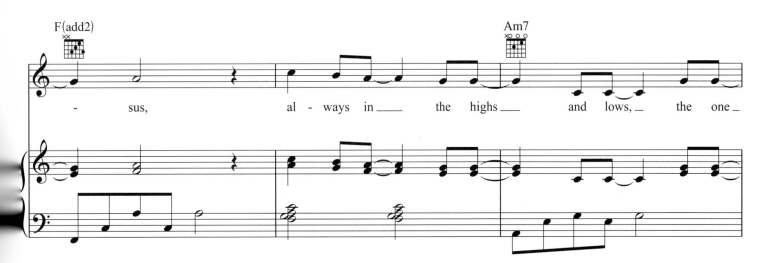

- sus, al - ways in ___ the highs ___ and lows, __ the one __

__ who goes __ be - fore ___ me. God ___ is in ___ this ___

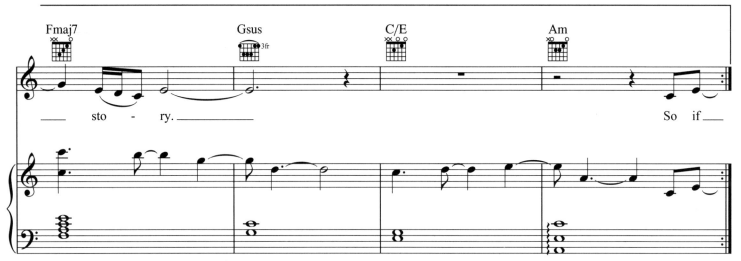

sto - ry. _____ So if ___

2
- me. God is in ___ this sto - ry. _____ If it

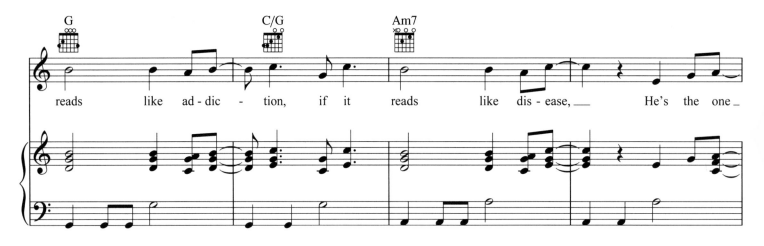

reads like ad - dic - tion, if it reads like dis - ease, ___ He's the one _

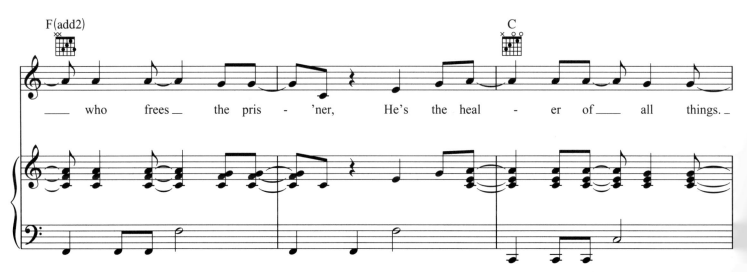

___ who frees ___ the pris - 'ner, He's the heal - er of ___ all things. _

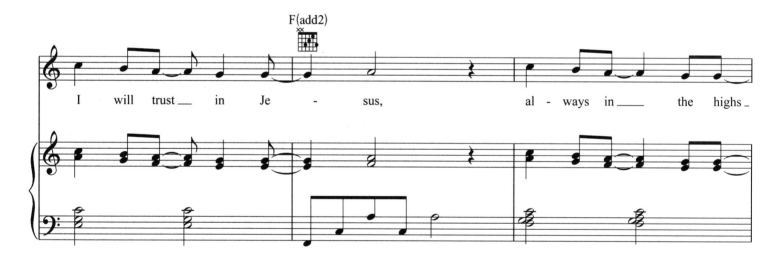

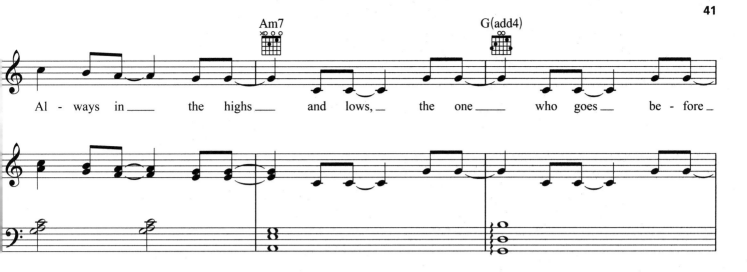

Al - ways in ___ the highs ___ and lows, ___ the one ___ who goes ___ be - fore ___

___ me. ___ God is in ___ this ___ sto - ry.

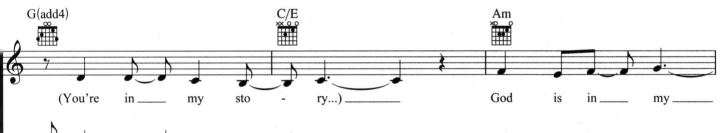

(You're in ___ my sto - ry...) ___ God is in ___ my ___

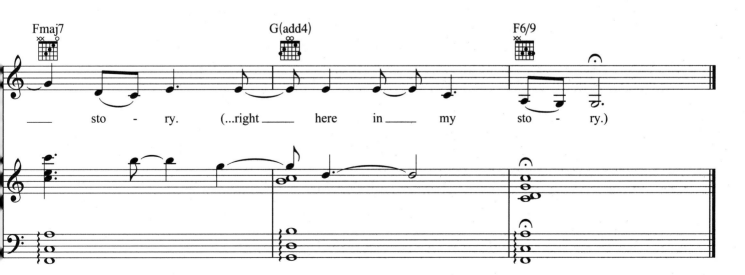

___ sto - ry. (...right ___ here in ___ my sto - ry.)

THE GOODNESS

Words and Music by TOBY McKEEHAN,
KYLE WILLIAMS, BRYAN FOWLER
and GABE PATILLO

*Recorded a half step lower.

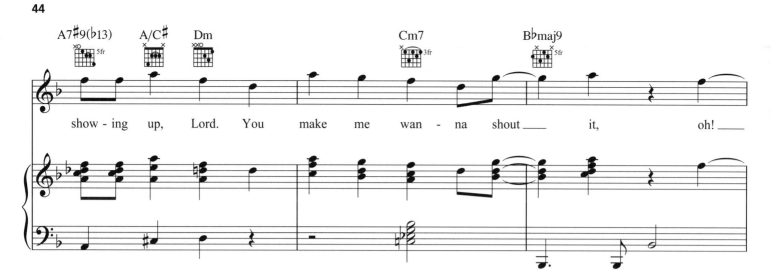

show-ing up, Lord. You make me wan-na shout ___ it, oh! ___

___ You're the good - ness in ___ my life. ___ And I'm-a tell You my

truth. __ They may come, they may go, You keep show-ing up, sure do.

Ain't no doubt a-bout ___ it: You are ___ the good - ness in ___ my life. _

To Coda

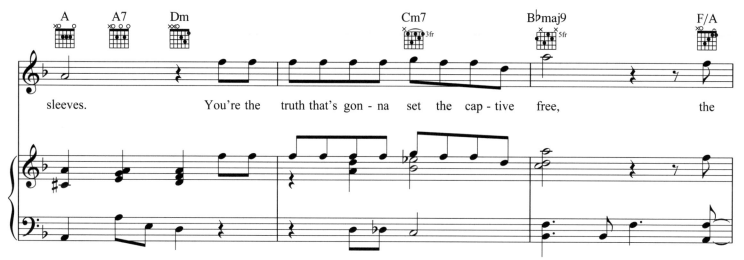

sleeves. You're the truth that's gon - na set the cap - tive free, the

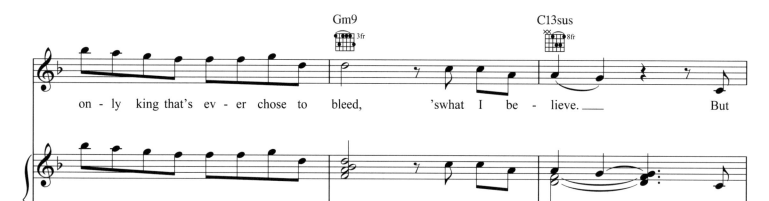

on - ly king that's ev - er chose to bleed, 'swhat I be - lieve. ___ But

they keep try - ing to make Your glo - ry fade. ___ But

D.S. al Coda

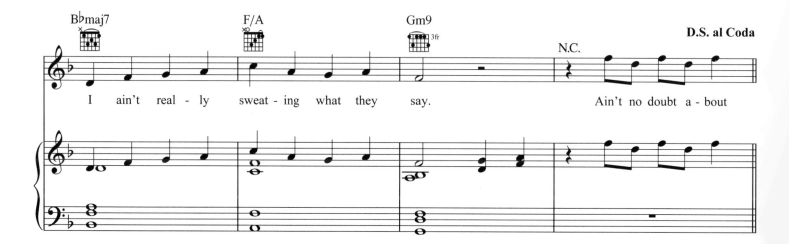

I ain't real - ly sweat - ing what they say. Ain't no doubt a - bout

Through the good ___ and the bad ___ and the ug-

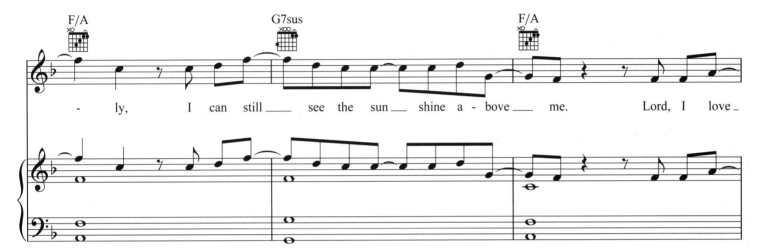

-ly, I can still ___ see the sun ___ shine a - bove ___ me. Lord, I love ___

___ all the ways ___ that You love ___ me. You're the good, ___

___ You're the good, ___ You're the good - ness. Through the good ___

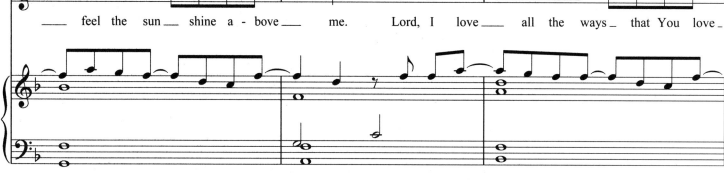

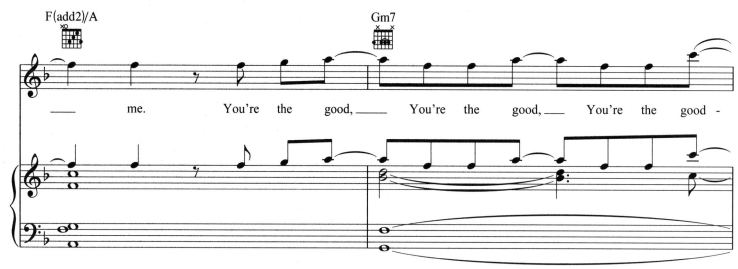

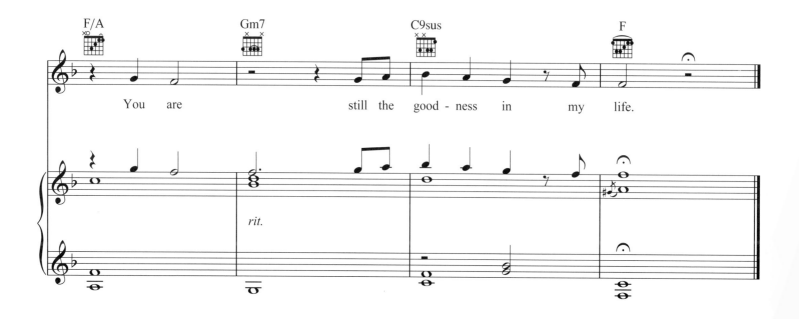

HYMN OF HEAVEN

Words and Music by PHIL WICKHAM,
BRIAN JOHNSON, BILL JOHNSON
and CHRIS DAVENPORT

Steady 4

How I long to breathe the air of heav - en, where pain is
breath we pray in des - per - a - tion, the songs of

gone and mer - cy fills the streets, to look up - on
faith we sang through doubt and fear, in the end

the One who bled to save me, and walk with Him
we'll see that it was worth it when He re - turns

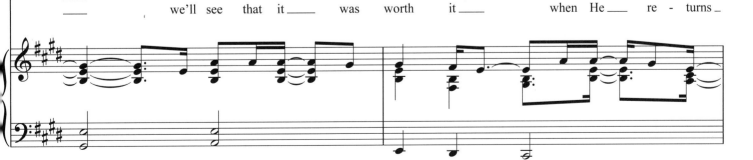

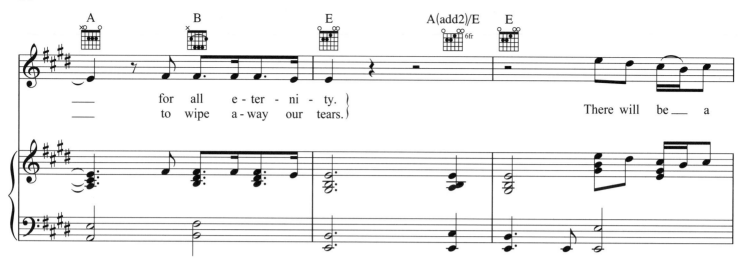

for all e-ter-ni-ty.
to wipe a-way our tears.
There will be __ a

day when all will bow __ be-fore __ Him. There will be __ a day when death will be __ no

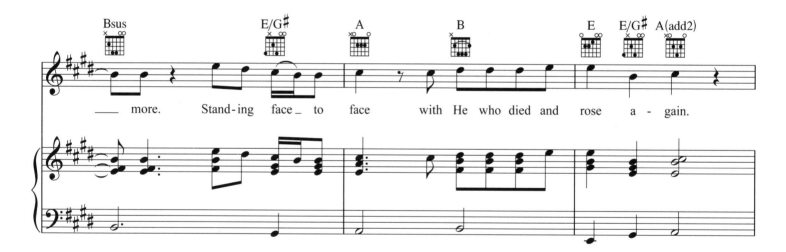

__ more. Stand-ing face __ to face with He who died and rose a-gain.

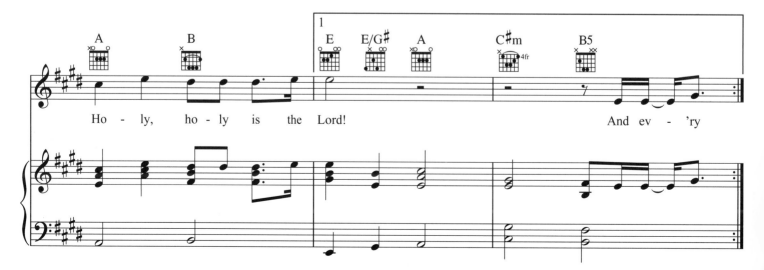

Ho-ly, ho-ly is the Lord! And ev-'ry

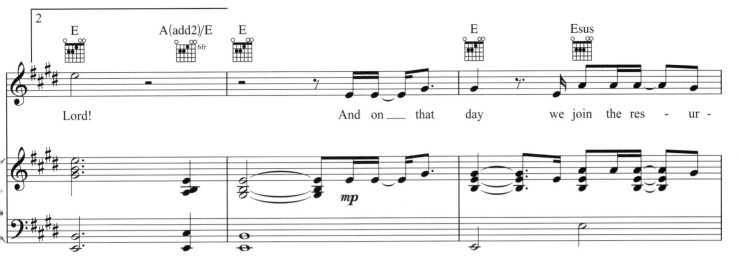

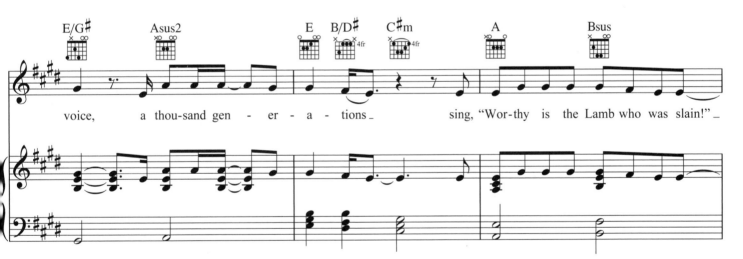

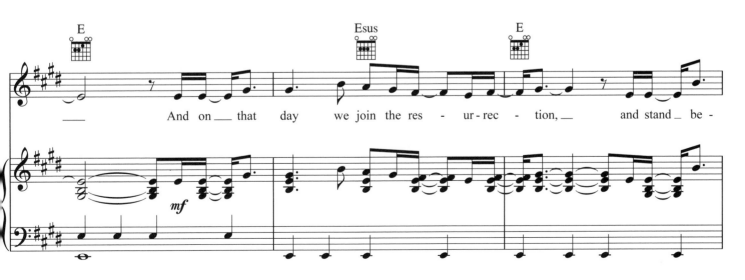

side the he-roes of ___ the faith. ___ With _ one voice, _ a thou-sand gen - er-

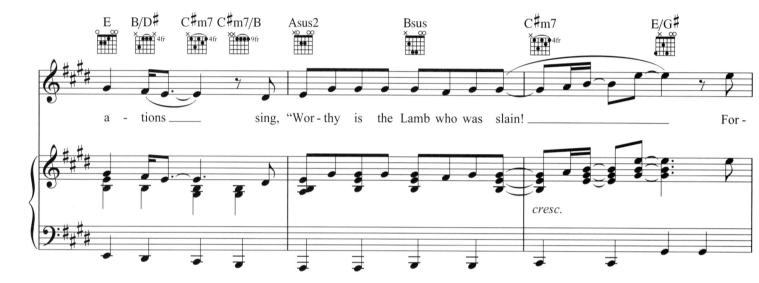

a - tions ___ sing, "Wor-thy is the Lamb who was slain! ___ For-

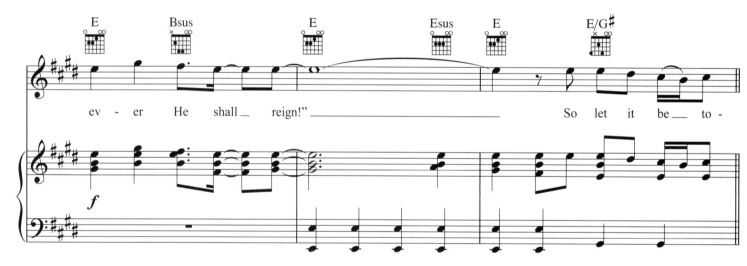

ev - er He shall _ reign!" ___ So let it be _ to-

day we shout the hymn _ of heav - en. With an-gels and _ the

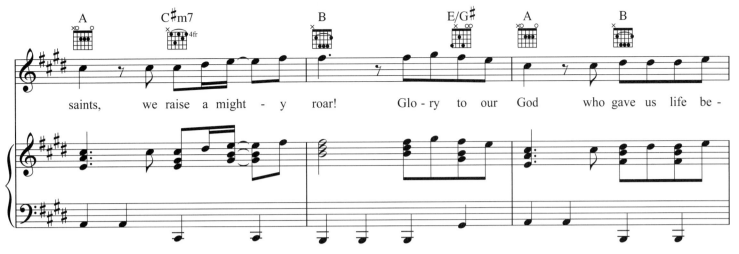

saints, we raise a might - y roar! Glo - ry to our God who gave us life be -

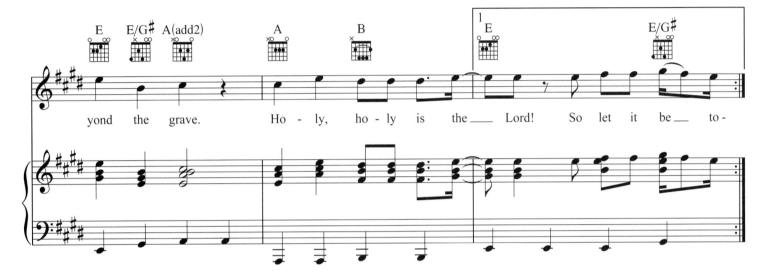

yond the grave. Ho - ly, ho - ly is the ___ Lord! So let it be ___ to -

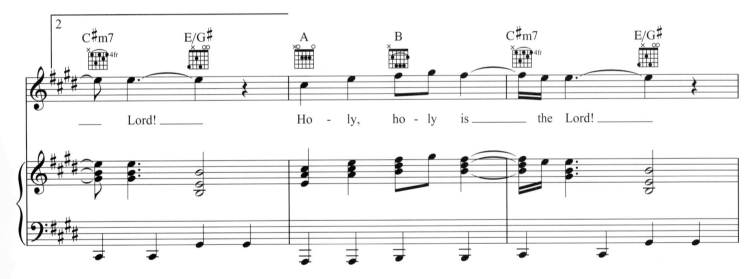

___ Lord! ___ Ho - ly, ho - ly is ___ the Lord! ___

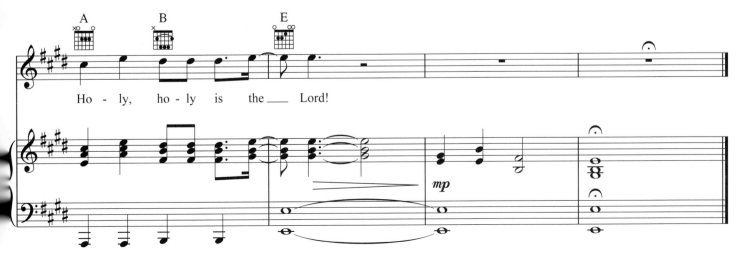

Ho - ly, ho - ly is the ___ Lord!

HOW FAR

Words and Music by MATTHEW WEST,
AJ PRUIS, TASHA LAYTON
and KEITH SMITH

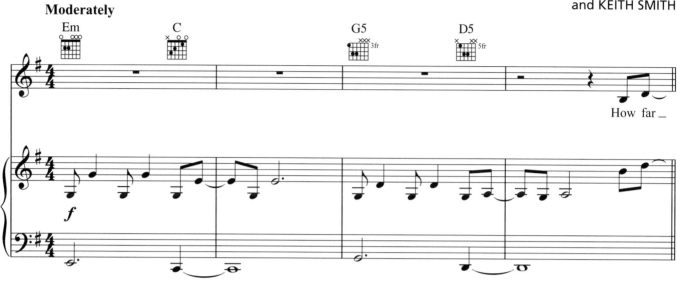

How far __

__ is too far? __ I thought I'd __ be there __ by now. __

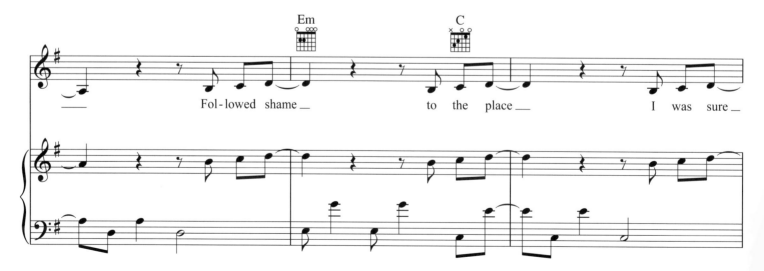

__ Fol-lowed shame __ to the place __ I was sure __

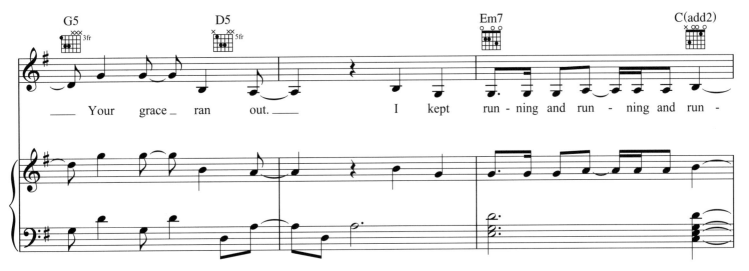

Your grace ___ ran out. ___ I kept run - ning and run - ning and run -

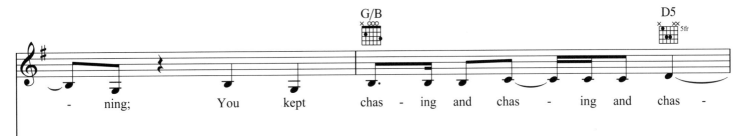

- ning; You kept chas - ing and chas - ing and chas -

- ing. A mil - lion miles ___ of my ___ mis - takes ___ still could -

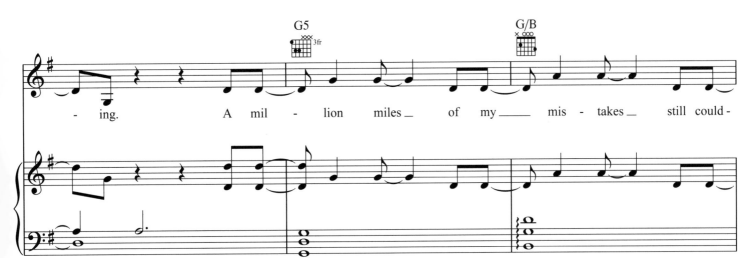

- n't keep ___ Your love ___ a - way. ___ How - ev - er far ___ a - way ___

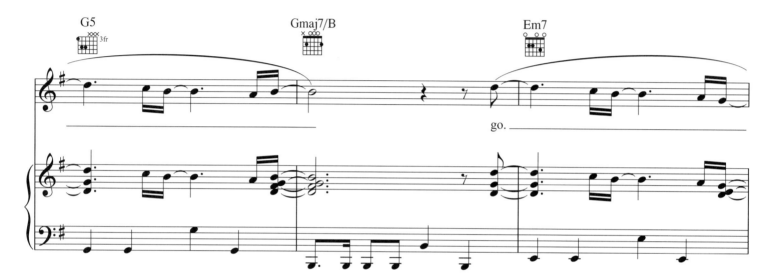

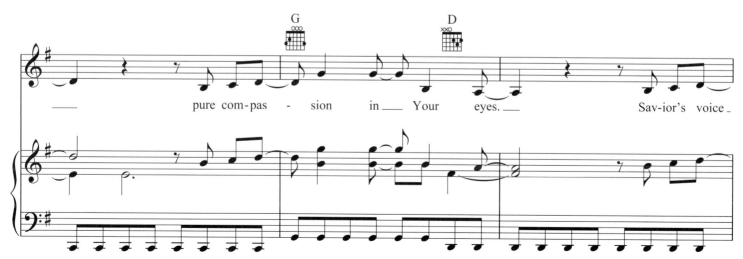

says to me, ___ "Time to come ___ back home, ___ my child." ___

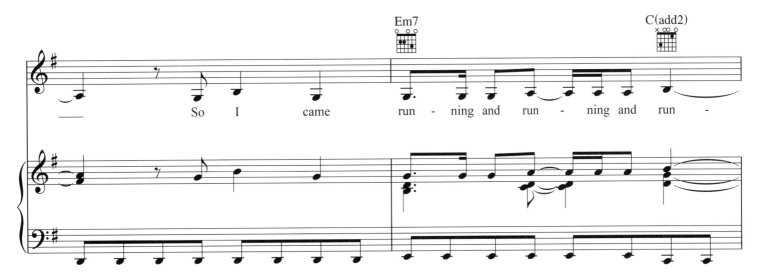

So I came run - ning and run - ning and run -

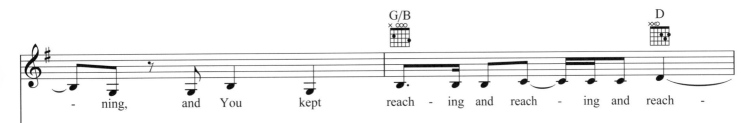

- ning, and You kept reach - ing and reach - ing and reach -

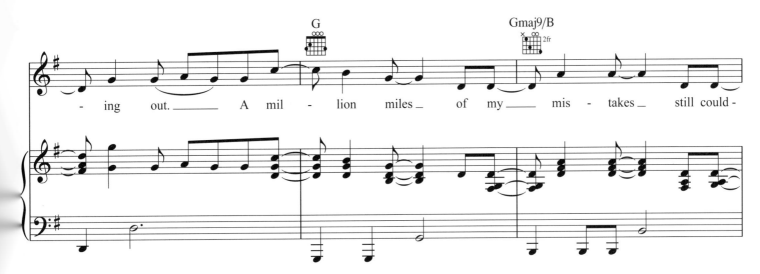

- ing out. ___ A mil - lion miles ___ of my ___ mis - takes ___ still could -

-n't keep __ Your love __ a - way. __ How - ev - er far __ a - way __

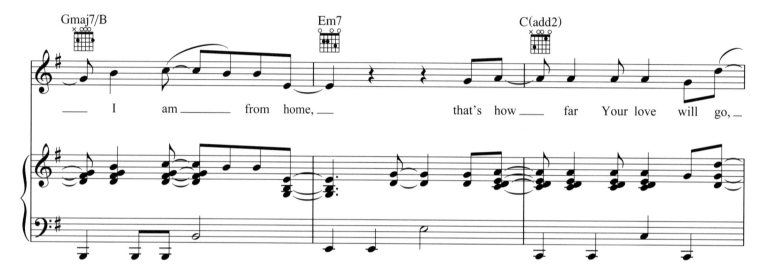

__ I am __ from home, __ that's how __ far Your love will go, __

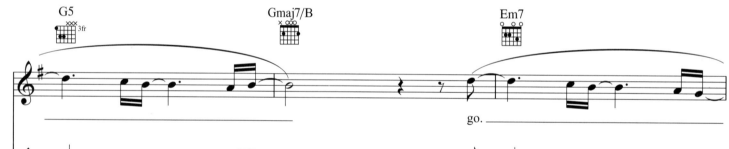

_____ go. __

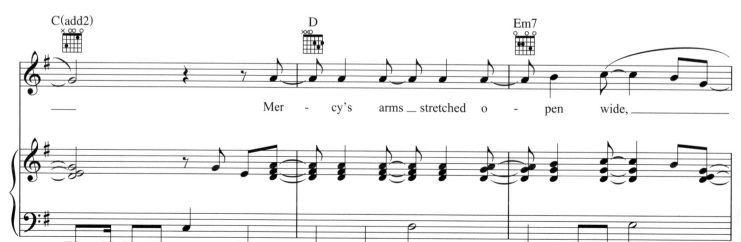

__ Mer - cy's arms __ stretched o - pen wide, __

You __ paid it all. __ What kind __ of love __ lays down

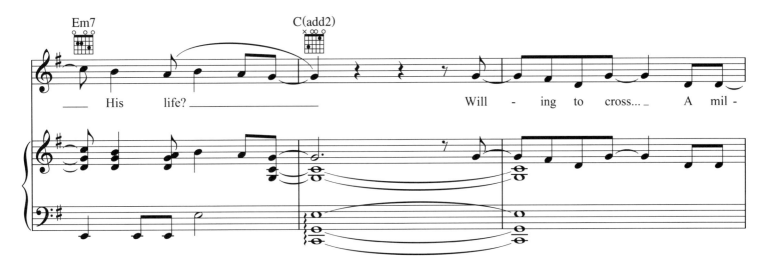

__ His life? _____ Will - ing to cross... _ A mil -

- lion miles __ of my __ mis - takes __ still could - n't keep __ Your love __

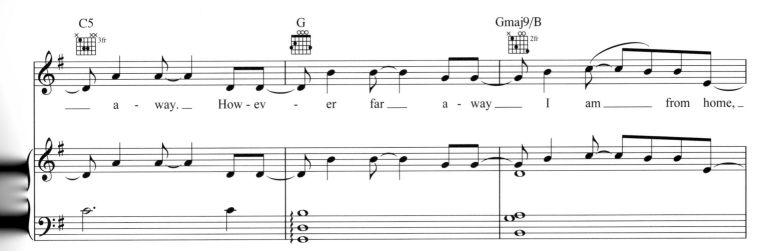

__ a - way. How - ev - er far __ a - way __ I am __ from home, __

that's how ___ far Your love will go. ___

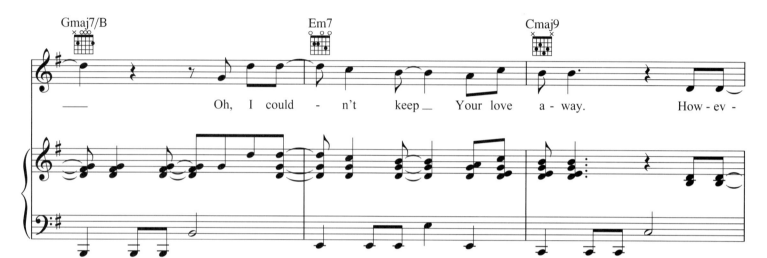

___ Oh, I could - n't keep ___ Your love a - way. How - ev -

- er far ___ a - way ___ I am ___ from home, ___

___ that's how ___ far Your love will go, ___

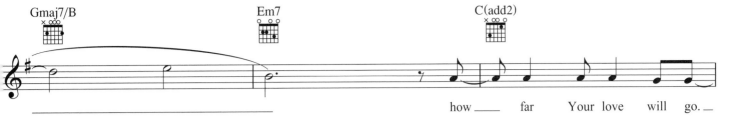

how ___ far Your love will go. ___

Arms stretched o - pen ___ wide, _____ that's how ___

___ far Your love will go. ___

That's how ___ far Your love will go. ___

IN JESUS NAME
(God of Possible)

Words and Music by KATY NICHOLE,
JEFF PARDO, ETHAN HULSE
and DAVID SPENCER

Moderately

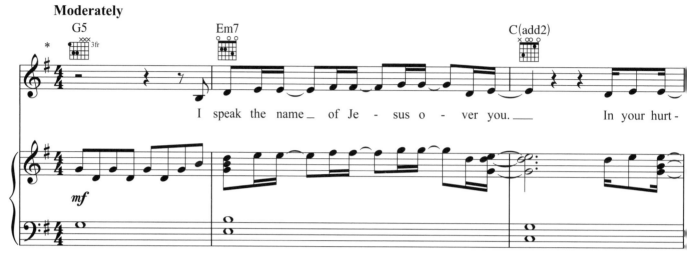

I speak the name of Je - sus o - ver you. In your hurt-

-ing, in your sor - row I will ask my God to move. I

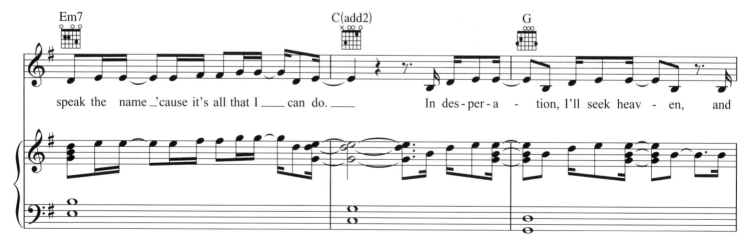

speak the name 'cause it's all that I can do. In des - per - a - tion, I'll seek heav - en, and

*Recorded a half step lower.

pray this for you. __ I pray for your heal - ing, __ that cir-cum-stanc-es would

change. I pray that the fear in-side would flee in Je-sus' __ name. I pray that a

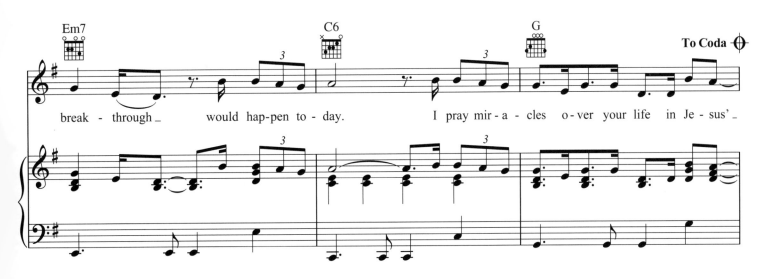

break - through __ would hap-pen to - day. I pray mir-a-cles o-ver your life in Je-sus' __

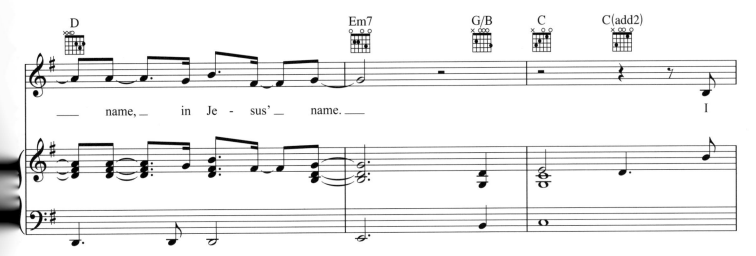

__ name, __ in Je-sus' __ name. __ I

speak the name __ of all __ au - thor - i - ty, ___ de - clar - ing bless-

- ings, ev - 'ry prom - ise He is faith - ful to ___ keep. __ I

speak the name __ no grave __ could ev - er hold. ___ He is great-

- er, He is strong - er, He's the God ___ of pos - si - ble. __ I pray for your

D.S. al Coda

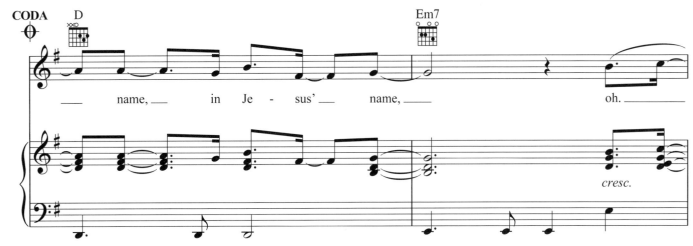

name, ___ in Je - sus' ___ name, ___ oh. ___

___ Come be - lieve ___ it, come re - ceive ___ it. ___ Oh, the pow -

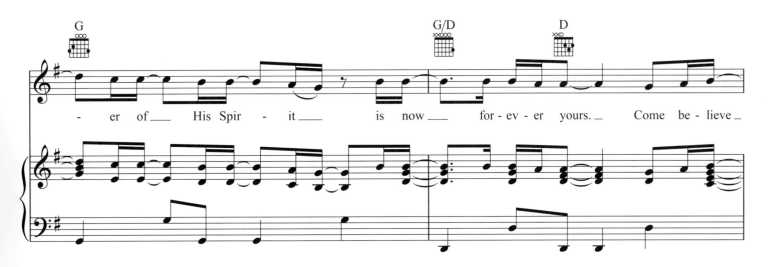

- er of ___ His Spir - it ___ is now ___ for - ev - er yours. ___ Come be - lieve ___

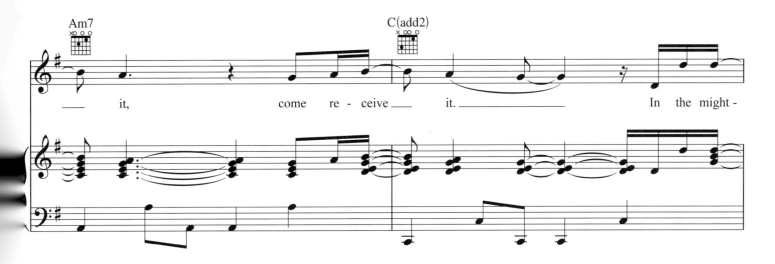

___ it, come re - ceive ___ it. ___ In the might -

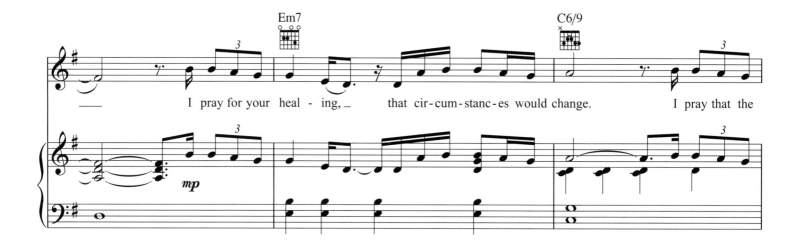

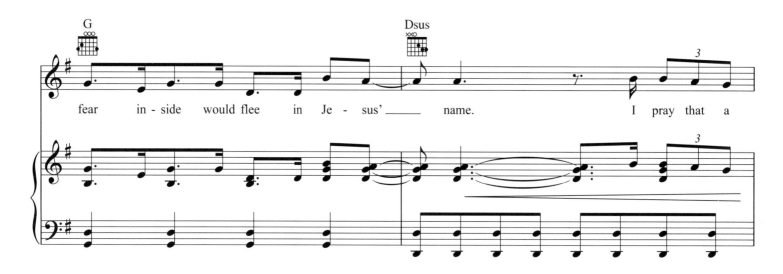

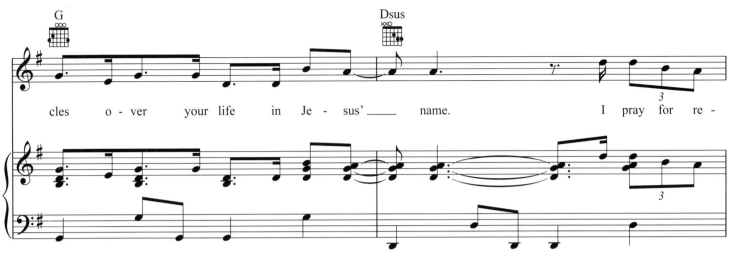

cles o - ver your life in Je - sus' ___ name. I pray for re -

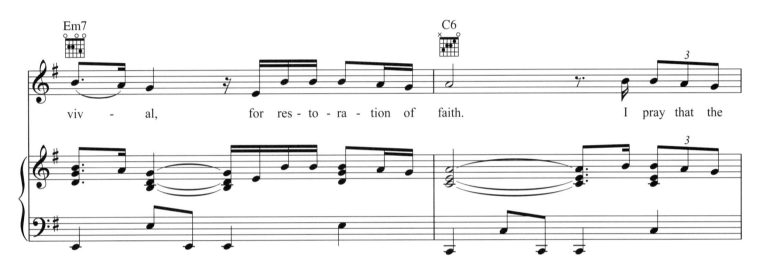

viv - al, for res - to - ra - tion of faith. I pray that the

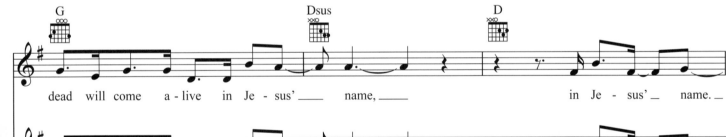

dead will come a - live in Je - sus' ___ name, ___ in Je - sus' ___ name. ___

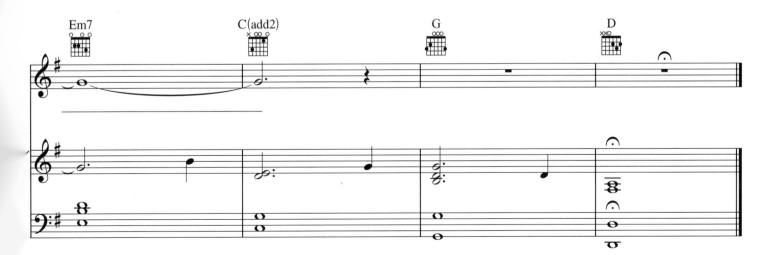

ME ON YOUR MIND

Words and Music by MATTHEW WEST,
ANNE WILSON and JEFF PARDO

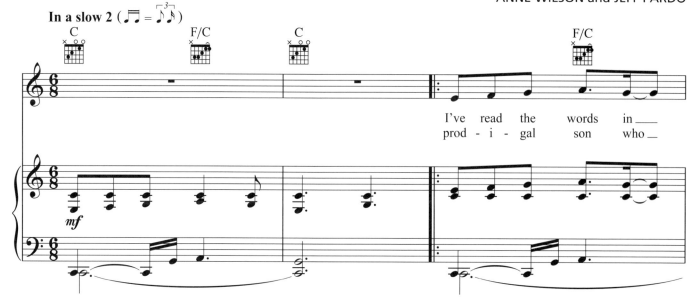

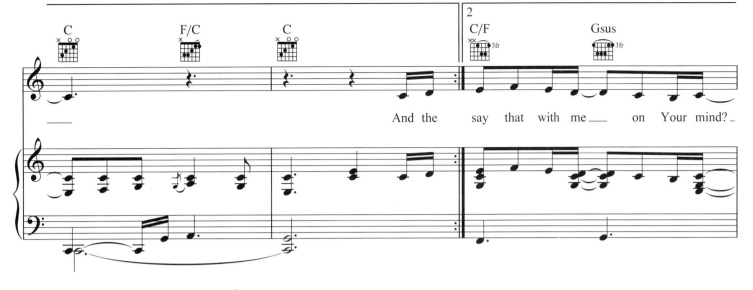

And the say that with me ___ on Your mind? ___

___ Who am I ___ that the King ___ of the world ___ would give one sin - gle thought ___

___ a - bout my bro - ken heart? ___ Who am I ___ that the God ___ of all

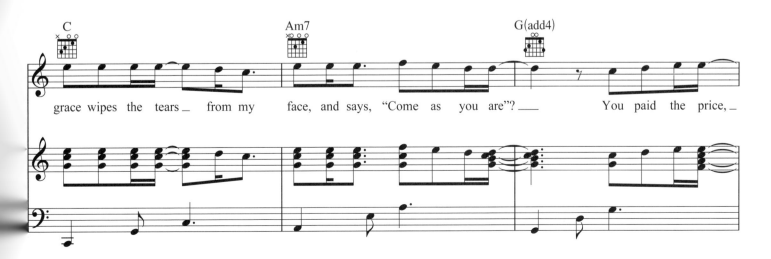

grace wipes the tears ___ from my face, and says, "Come as you are"? ___ You paid the price, ___

You took the cross, ___ You gave Your life. ___ And You did it all ___

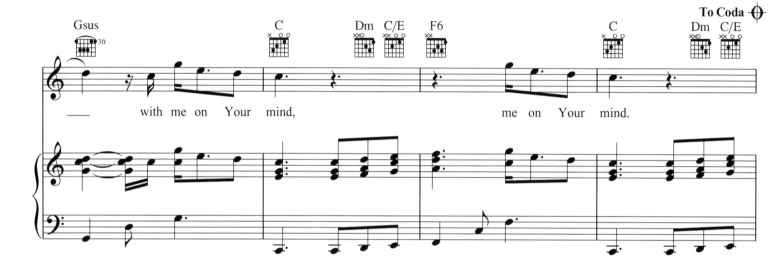

___ with me on Your mind,   me on Your mind.

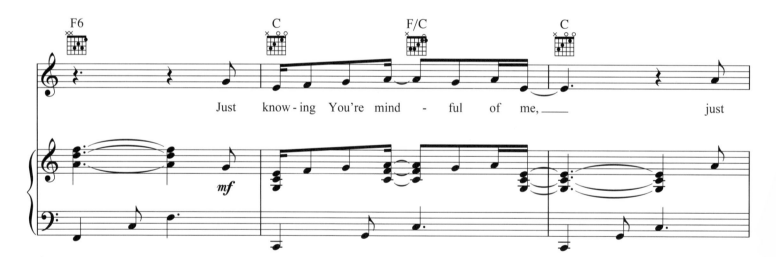

Just know-ing You're mind - ful of me, ___ just

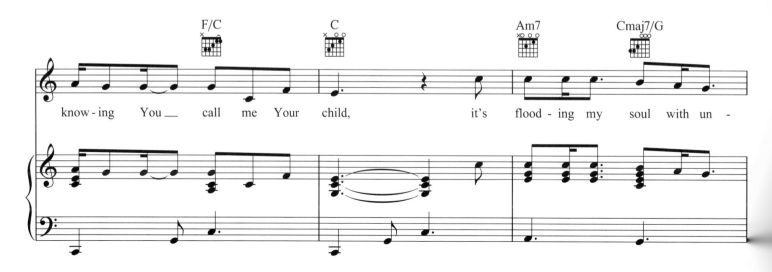

know-ing You ___ call me Your child,   it's flood-ing my soul with un -

D.S. al Coda

speak - a - ble hope. Thank You, Lord, that it's me on Your ____ mind. Who am I ___

CODA

Oh, _____ thank You, Je - sus.

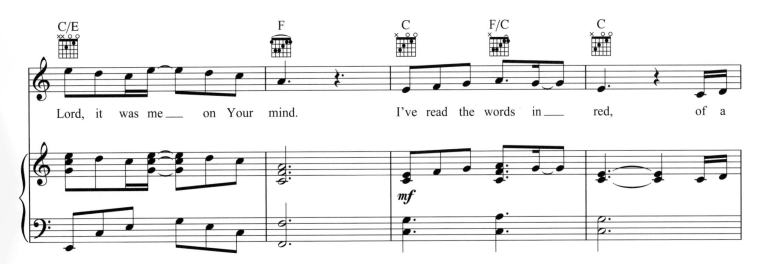

Lord, it was me __ on Your mind. I've read the words in __ red, of a

heav - en - ly home on _____ high. _ You're pre - par - ing a place _ where the sor -

- row's e - rased. _ And when I stand be - fore _ You, I'll _ find, all a - long, _

_ it was me _ on Your _ mind. Who am I _ that the King _ of the world _

_ would give one sin - gle thought _ a - bout my bro - ken heart? _ Who am I _

_ that the God _ of all grace wipes the tears _ from my face, and says, "Come as you _

SEE ME THROUGH IT

Words and Music by BRANDON HEATH,
KYLE WILLIAMS, RAN JACKSON
and HEATHER MORGAN

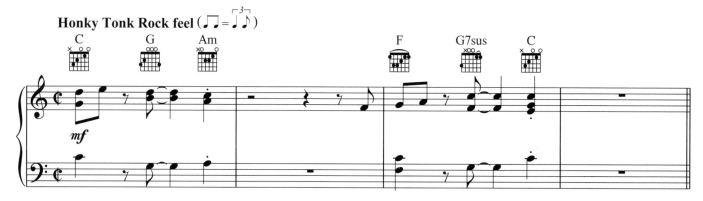

Things are get - ting real. Je - sus, take the wheel. On - ly way I'm

When the sky ___ falls, who'm I gon - na call? The One who put it

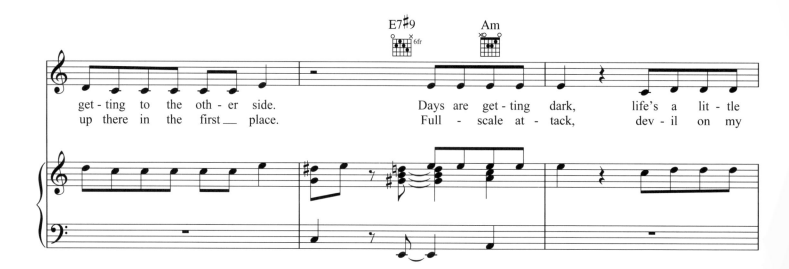

get - ting to the oth - er side. Days are get - ting dark, life's a lit - tle

up there in the first ___ place. Full - scale at - tack, dev - il on my

hard.   Blind - ed, but I'm try - ing not to lose sight.)
back.   Bet - ter lace 'em up and go put on my game face.)   I don't got __

__ this. I know You got __ this, yeah, yeah, yeah.   And I be - lieve __

__ it be - fore I see __ it, yeah, yeah, yeah.   I know You're gon - na

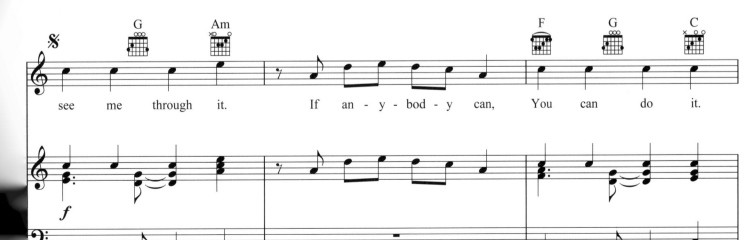

see me through it.   If an - y - bod - y can, You can do it.

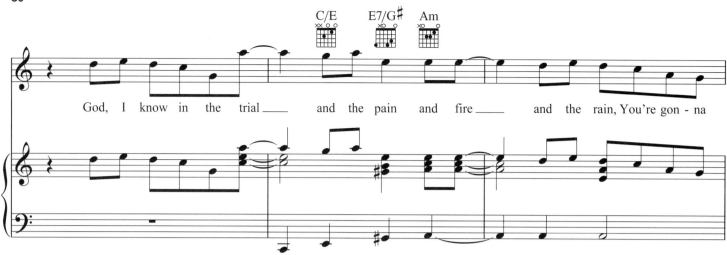

God, I know in the trial ___ and the pain and fire ___ and the rain, You're gon - na

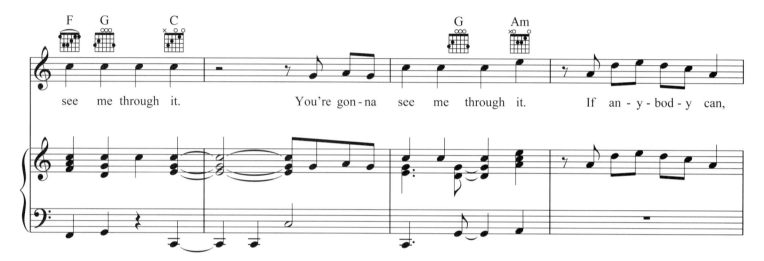

see me through it. You're gon - na see me through it. If an - y - bod - y can,

You can do it. And when - ev - er my hope ___ runs a - way, You ___

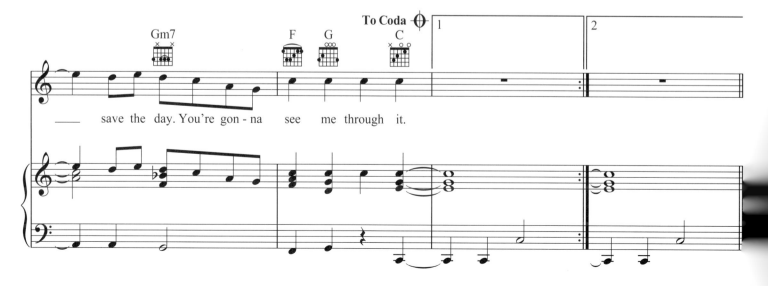

___ save the day. You're gon - na see me through it.

cues: 2nd time only

Our God is big-ger than all our prob-lems the on-ly One who knows how to solve 'em. So if you're sit-ting in the back, rock bot-tom, prayers in the

air if you got 'em. | air if you got 'em,

D.S. al Coda

CODA

mf

Yeah, __ yeah, yeah. __ I know You're gon-na see me through it. _____

THEN CHRIST CAME

Words and Music by BART MILLARD,
PHIL WICKHAM, DAVID LEONARD
and JASON INGRAM

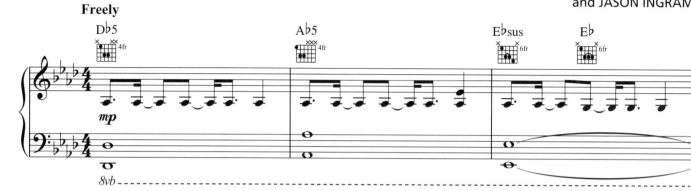

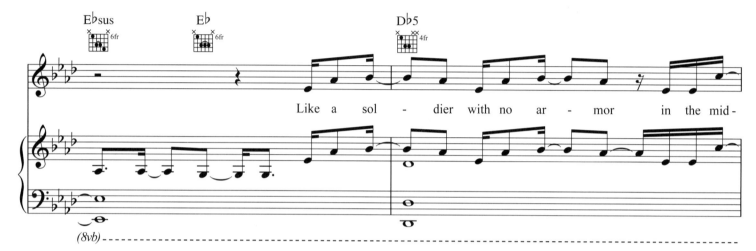

Like a sol-dier with no ar-mor in the mid-

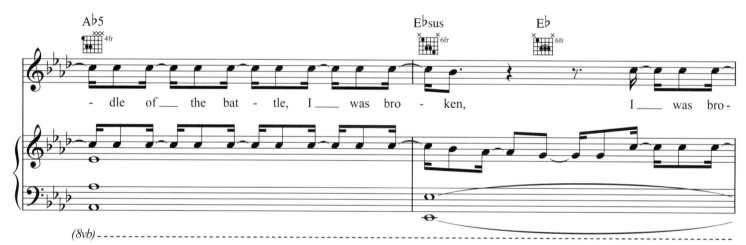

-dle of ___ the bat-tle, I ___ was bro-ken, I ___ was bro-

-ken. It was on-ly get-ting dark-er in the val-

that I ___ could ev - er real - ly mat - ter, ___ ev - er mat -

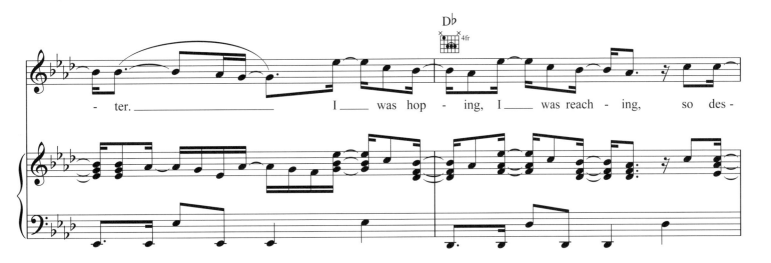

- ter. ___ I ___ was hop - ing, I ___ was reach - ing, so des -

- p'rate for ___ my soul ___ to find ___ its Sav - ior. ___ I need a Sav -

- ior. ___ Then Christ ___ came, ___ chang - ing ev - 'ry - thing. ___

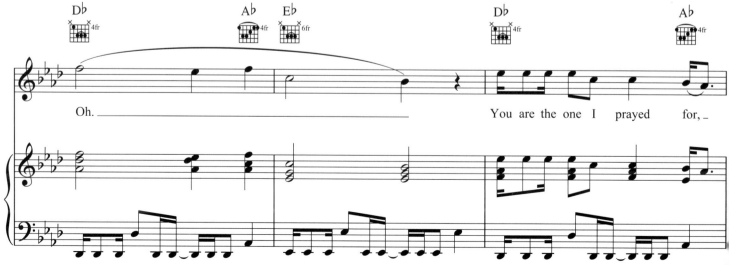

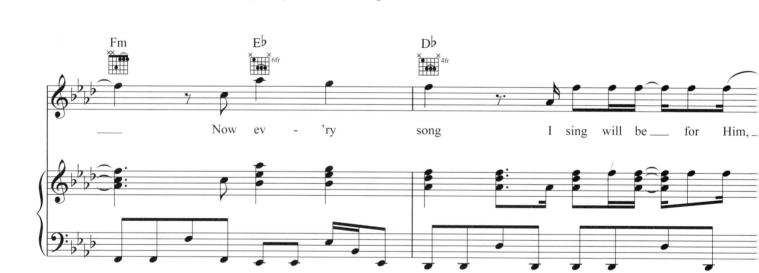

You are the one I prayed ___ for, ___ You are the one I was made ___ for. ___

Hal - le - lu - jah. Je - sus, You gave me pur - pose. ___

Je - sus, You told me I'm worth it. ___ Hal - le - lu - jah. _____

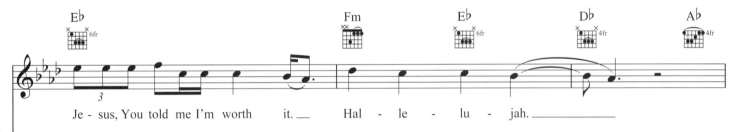

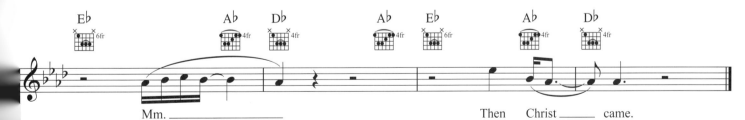

Mm. _____ Then Christ ___ came.

WEARY TRAVELER

Words and Music by ANDREW PRUIS,
MATTHEW WEST and JORDAN ST. CYR

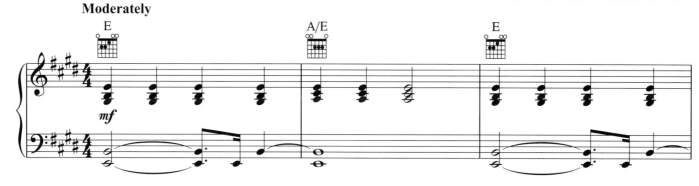

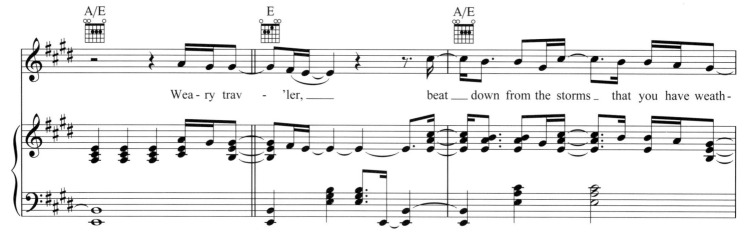

Wea-ry trav - 'ler, _____ beat ___ down from the storms ___ that you have weath-

- ered. _____ Feels like this road ___ just might ___ go on ___ for - ev-

- er. _____ Car-ry on. _____ You keep on giv - ing, _____ but

ev - 'ry day __ this world __ just keeps __ on tak - ing. __ Your

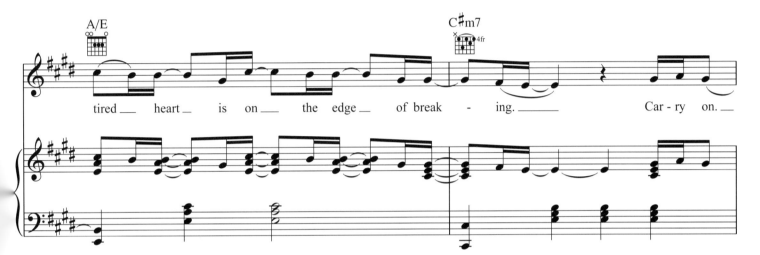

tired __ heart __ is on __ the edge __ of break - ing. __ Car - ry on. __

__ Wea - ry trav - 'ler, rest - less soul. You were

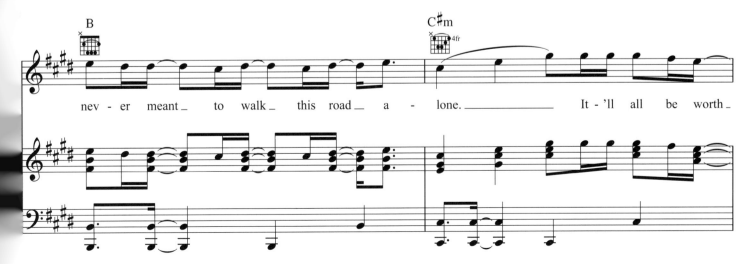

nev - er meant __ to walk __ this road a - lone. __ It - 'll all be worth __

it, so just hold on. ___ Wea-ry trav - 'ler, ___ you won't ___ be wea-ry long. ___

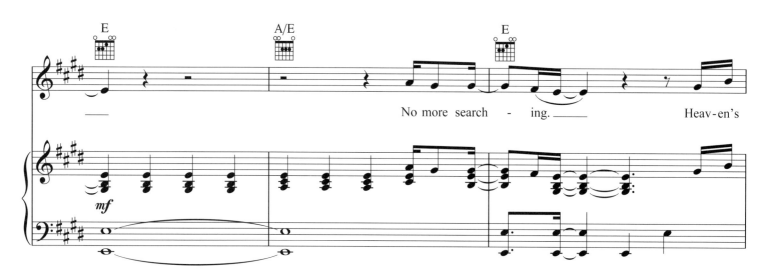

___ No more search - ing. ___ Heav-en's

heal - ing's gon - na find ___ where all the hurt ___ is. ___ When Je - sus

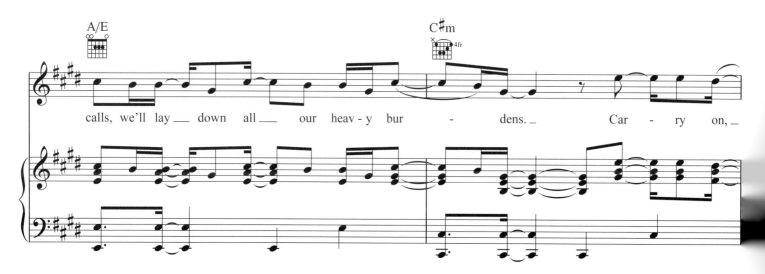

calls, we'll lay ___ down all ___ our heav-y bur - dens. ___ Car - ry on, ___

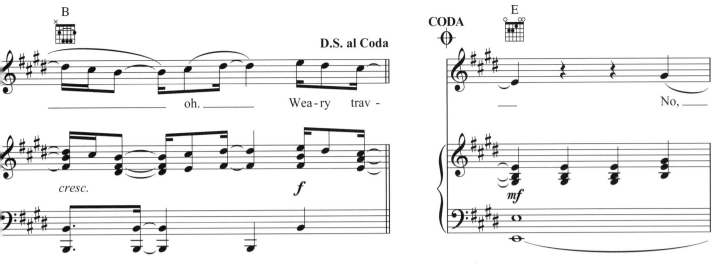

oh. Wea-ry trav-

you won't be wea-ry long, _____ you won't be wea-ry long.

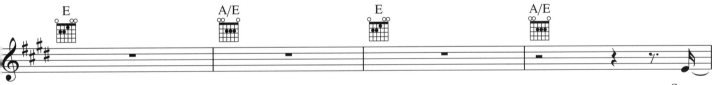

Some-

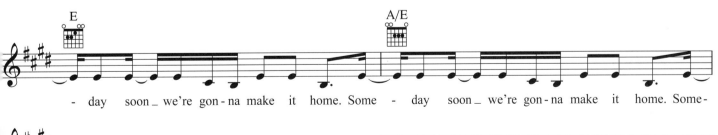

- day soon_ we're gon-na make it home. Some - day soon_ we're gon-na make it home. Some-

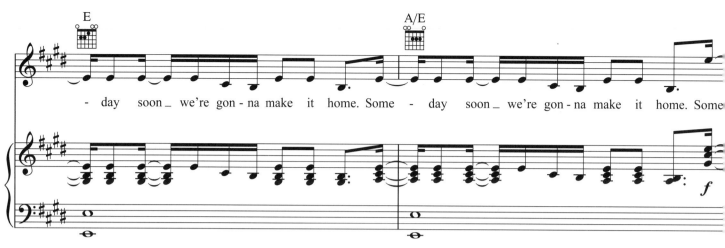

-day soon we're gon-na make it home. Some - day soon we're gon-na make it home. Some

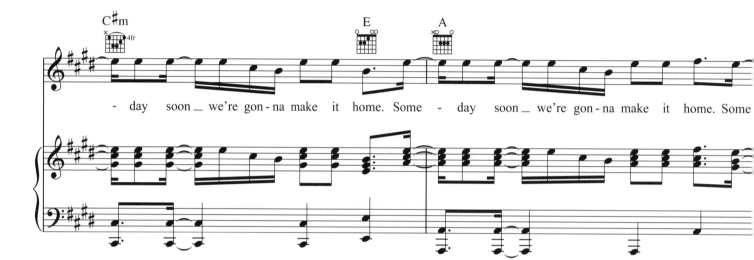

-day soon we're gon-na make it home. Some - day soon we're gon-na make it home. Some

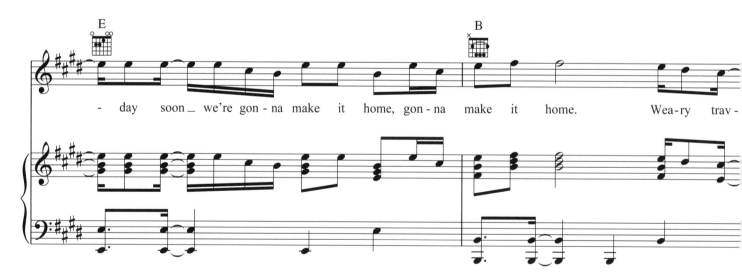

-day soon we're gon-na make it home, gon - na make it home. Wea-ry trav-

-'ler, rest-less soul. You were nev - er meant to walk this road a -

lone._____ It - 'll all be worth _ it, so just hold

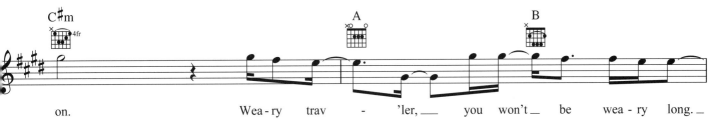

on. Wea - ry trav - 'ler, _ you won't _ be wea - ry long. _

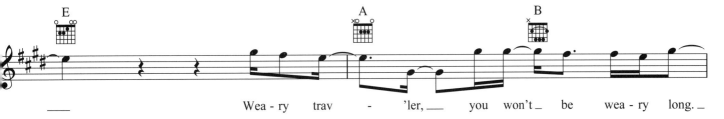

__ Wea - ry trav - 'ler, _ you won't _ be wea - ry long. _

Wea - ry trav - 'ler, _ you won't _ be wea - ry long. _

The Best
PRAISE & WORSHIP
Songbooks for Piano

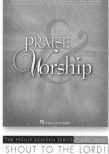
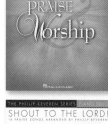

Above All
THE PHILLIP KEVEREN SERIES
15 beautiful praise song piano solo arrangements by Phillip Keveren. Includes: Above All • Agnus Dei • Breathe • Draw Me Close • He Is Exalted • I Stand in Awe • Step by Step • We Fall Down • You Are My King (Amazing Love) • and more.
00311024 Piano Solo..................................$14.99

Blended Worship Piano Collection
Songs include: Amazing Grace (My Chains Are Gone) • Be Thou My Vision • Cornerstone • Fairest Lord Jesus • Great Is Thy Faithfulness • How Great Is Our God • I Will Rise • Joyful, Joyful, We Adore Thee • Lamb of God • Majesty • Open the Eyes of My Heart • Praise to the Lord, the Almighty • Shout to the Lord • 10,000 Reasons (Bless the Lord) • Worthy Is the Lamb • Your Name • and more.
00293528 Piano Solo $17.99

Blessings
THE PHILLIP KEVEREN SERIES
Phillip Keveren delivers another stellar collection of piano solo arrangements perfect for any reverent or worship setting: Blessed Be Your Name • Blessings • Cornerstone • Holy Spirit • This Is Amazing Grace • We Believe • Your Great Name • Your Name • and more.
00156601 Piano Solo $14.99

The Best Praise & Worship Songs Ever
80 all-time favorites: Awesome God • Breathe • Days of Elijah • Here I Am to Worship • I Could Sing of Your Love Forever • Open the Eyes of My Heart • Shout to the Lord • We Bow Down • dozens more.
00311057 P/V/G...................................$29.99

Contemporary Worship Duets
arr. Bill Wolaver
Contains 8 powerful songs carefully arranged by Bill Wolaver as duets for intermediate-level players: Agnus Dei • Be unto Your Name • He Is Exalted • Here I Am to Worship • I Will Rise • The Potter's Hand • Revelation Song • Your Name.
00290593 Piano Duets $10.99

The Best of Passion
Over 40 worship favorites featuring the talents of David Crowder, Matt Redman, Chris Tomlin, and others. Songs include: Always • Awakening • Blessed Be Your Name • Jesus Paid It All • My Heart Is Yours • Our God • 10,000 Reasons (Bless the Lord) • and more.
00101888 P/V/G $19.99

Praise & Worship Duets
THE PHILLIP KEVEREN SERIES
8 worshipful duets by Phillip Keveren: As the Deer • Awesome God • Give Thanks • Great Is the Lord • Lord, I Lift Your Name on High • Shout to the Lord • There Is a Redeemer • We Fall Down.
00311203 Piano Duet $14.99

Shout to the Lord!
THE PHILLIP KEVEREN SERIES
14 favorite praise songs, including: As the Deer • El Shaddai • Give Thanks • Great Is the Lord • How Beautiful • More Precious Than Silver • Oh Lord, You're Beautiful • A Shield About Me • Shine, Jesus, Shine • Shout to the Lord • Thy Word • and more.
00310699 Piano Solo $16.99

Sunday Solos in the Key of C
CLASSIC & CONTEMPORARY WORSHIP SONGS
22 C-major selections, including: Above All • Good Good Father • His Name Is Wonderful • Holy Spirit • Lord, I Need You • Reckless Love • What a Beautiful Name • You Are My All in All • and more.
00301044 Piano Solo $14.99

The Chris Tomlin Collection – 2nd Edition
15 songs from one of the leading artists and composers in Contemporary Christian music, including the favorites: Amazing Grace (My Chains Are Gone) • Holy Is the Lord • How Can I Keep from Singing • How Great Is Our God • Jesus Messiah • Our God • We Fall Down • and more.
00306951 P/V/G $17.99

Top 25 Worship Songs
25 contemporary worship hits includes: Glorious Day (Passion) • Good, Good Father (Chris Tomlin) • Holy Spirit (Francesca Battistelli) • King of My Heart (John Mark & Sarah McMillan) • The Lion and the Lamb (Big Daddy Weave) • Reckless Love (Cory Asbury) • 10,000 Reasons (Matt Redman) • This Is Amazing Grace (Phil Wickham) • What a Beautiful Name (Hillsong Worship) • and more.
00288610 P/V/G $19.99

Top Worship Downloads
20 of today's chart-topping Christian hits, including Cornerstone • Forever Reign • Great I Am • Here for You • Lord, I Need You • My God • Never Once • One Thing Remains (Your Love Never Fails) • Your Great Name • and more.
00120870 P/V/G $16.95

The World's Greatest Praise Songs
Shawnee Press
This is a unique and useful collection of 50 of the very best praise titles of the last three decades. Includes: Above All • Forever • Here I Am to Worship • I Could Sing of Your Love Forever • Open the Eyes of My Heart • and so many more.
35022891 P/V/G $19.9

HAL•LEONARD®
www.halleonard.com
P/V/G = Piano/Vocal/Guitar Arrangements

Prices, contents, and availability subject to change without notice.

122